The Way to Write

JOHN FAIRFAX
and JOHN MOAT

Foreword by Ted Hughes

ST. MARTIN'S PRESS
NEW YORK

For three mentors
G.B., J.H.B. and R.G-H.

And for E.W.W.
who opened the door

Library of Congress Cataloging in Publication Data

Fairfax, John, 1930-
    The way to write.

    1. Creative writing.   I. Moat, John.   II. Title.
PN187.F3   808′.042   81-18431
ISBN 0-312-85832-9   AACR2
ISBN 0-312-85833-7 (pbk.)
ISBN 0-312-85834-5 (ppk.)

Contents

Note

A glimpse at the history of literary criticism will show how little agreement there has ever been about the distinction between Poetry and Prose. Happily it is not a debate that need tax us because, with one or two minor exceptions, our concern is with the effective use of language as it is applicable to virtually any discipline of imaginative writing.

If it is that we draw most frequently from poetry for our illustrations, this does not reveal a greater interest in the writing of verse, merely it confesses where, in our store, the best illustrations were to be found.

J.F./J.M.
1980

Acknowledgements

The authors and publishers gratefully acknowledge the following for permission to reproduce extracts of prose and poems quoted in this book. Every effort has been made to trace the copyright holders, but, should there be any omissions in this respect, we apologise and shall be pleased to make the appropriate acknowledgement in any future editions.

A.E. Houseman: 'Lovliest of trees, the cherry now' by permission of The Society of Authors as the literary representative of the Estate of A.E. Houseman and Jonathan Cape Ltd., publishers of A.E. Houseman's *Collected Poems*.

Dylan Thomas: 'This bread I break' from *Collected Poems* by permission of the Trustees for the copyright of the late Dylan Thomas.

Gerard Manley Hopkins: *The Journals and Papers of Gerard Manley Hopkins* by permission of Oxford University Press.

Anne Sexton: 'Pain for a Daughter' from *Live or Die* by permission of A.D. Peters & Co Ltd.

Brian Patten: 'Diary Poem' from *Notes to the Hurrying Man* by permission of George Allen & Unwin.

Wilfred Owen: 'Anthem for a Doomed Youth' from *The Collected Poems of Wilfred Owen* by permission of the Owen Estate and Chatto & Windus Ltd.

James Stephens: 'In the Poppyfield' from *Collected Poems* by permission of Mrs Iris Wise and Macmillan, London and Basingstoke.

Robert Frost: 'Bereft' from *The Poetry of Robert Frost* edited by Edward Connery Latham by permission of the Estate of Robert Frost, Edward Connery Latham and Jonathan Cape Ltd.

Roger McGough: 'Fight of the Year' from *Watchwords* by permission of Roger McGough and Jonathan Cape Ltd.

Foreword by Ted Hughes

These chapters have grown naturally out of the work the authors have done with apprentice writers, on the courses given by The Arvon Foundation, over the last twelve years.

Since The Arvon Foundation provides the living context of almost everything they have to say, perhaps it would be as well to start by explaining a little of what it is and how it began.

John Moat and John Fairfax, the two authors of this book, invented it. They had come to feel (like many another) that the conventional methods of teaching English are unsatisfactory and, except where they are adapted by some exceptional teacher, fail to give students any guidance in the art of writing well, or any real idea of what makes creative language live, of how literature is made and why it is important, or of the fact that it is students who grow eventually into the people who produce all these books. John Moat and John Fairfax felt they knew what was wrong, and it seemed to them they knew how to correct it. Twelve years ago, all they asked for was a group of students who wanted to learn about writing. So they got them. They put their faith to the practical test, and organized a five day course.

Their idea was simple. It was: to gather about fourteen young people who were interested enough to make the effort, and two writers, in a secluded house, where all would live together for five days, working at writing. The only 'instruction' given would be what rose directly out of that involvement — the apprentice working, and the master guiding him as he worked, showing him how to work, helping him to work.

There is a Japanese proverb: 'Don't study an art, practice it.' And Sir Francis Bacon wrote: 'Example is a globe of precepts.' And these were the main working principles: practice from the apprentice, example from the master; that was all there was to it, plus the five day concentration on a common purpose, and seclusion.

John Fairfax and John Moat tutored the first course themselves. The students all came from mid-Devon and only one or two of them had made any attempt to write 'creatively' before. As it happened, I looked in on that launching of what was to become The Arvon

Foundation, and for several reasons I was made to remember it.

Some months before John Moat had visited me and outlined his plan, hoping that I would be interested and perhaps agree to be a tutor on one of the proposed courses. I daresay my reaction dismayed him, because as I recall I told him more or less outright that I thought the scheme was unworkable. It was the first time we had met. I think if I had known better what an unusual character I was listening to, I would have answered less definitely. Little did I suspect how dramatically my opinion of his idea was going to be reversed.

But at the time I simply felt he was wrong, and my negative was quite confident.

Before I say any more, I would like to dwell a little on that negative of mine, because it is not only mine. What exactly lay behind it? I have often had cause to ask myself this, because over the subsequent years, in my busy promotion of Arvon, I have again and again met that instant negative coming from others. Not a reasoned negative, but an automatic one — as if it crystallized, at a touch, out of a supersaturated solution.

What is particularly curious to me about my response, when I think of it now, is that I had quite strong reasons to say yes. Unlike many writers, I was a confirmed believer in 'poetic schools'. The notion of some modern version of the ancient Irish poetic schools, as evidence of them has come down to us, makes a deep appeal. That compulsory learning of a large body of traditional material, the incessant discipline in production, the methodical mobilizing and training of every scrap of potential, the nursing of artistic standards as sacred — at least — as athletic record performance: all that certainly grips the imagination. And, however rudimentary, what John Moat proposed was surely the seed of something that might grow a branch that way, some day.

Also, I had seen one form of the 'master' and 'apprentice' relationship working successfully in the United States. At quite close quarters I watched Robert Lowell's writing classes transform Anne Sexton from a housewife who had written a few undistinguished lines but who wanted to learn how to write better, into a remarkable author able to express, overwhelmingly, all that she was. And I watched the same classes supervise crucial changes in Sylvia Plath's writing. Almost every young American writer I met had worked — in just that 'apprentice' role — with some chosen 'master'. Robert Lowell himself had sought out Crowe Ransome and Allen Tate — so determined that he even pitched his tent on Tate's lawn, and lived there. I had marvelled — not without some envy — at the range and energy and generosity, yes, and the seriousness of discussion between American writers and students.

And I had felt the unselfconscious release of it, the charged positive atmosphere, the willingness to let the other man go his own way, the assumption that the greatest things are still to be done.

And what John Moat proposed surely pointed in the same direction.

My negative was so prompt, I think now, because I held a fixed, deeply sceptical preconception of what the English temperament would make of such an idea. And my first reference, for certain, was the usual English response to the idea of American Creative Writing classes. I had met it too often to doubt it. And that response is, almost inevitably, dismissive, and usually derisive too.

To go no further, to examine that reaction alone, leads immediately into a whole web of attitudes — commonly secreted but rarely interrogated — which all seem to share one decisive accent, and it is a negative accent: negative towards any deliberate cultivation of excellence, negative towards the methodical release of creative energy, negative towards enthusiasm, negative towards the future.

It would be an interesting exercise to search out the history and rise to power — even political power — of these attitudes, in our English life. It is a depressing exercise — but still interesting — to follow out their consequences, which amount to more than the amateurism and gentility, of which we so often accuse ourselves, though they supply some of the masks. Those attitudes do have real power: witness the plight of Education itself, which is the result of deliberate political decision. Education is a natural victim of the deadly negative, being the most essential of all our industries, with the most vital national product of all (future brains, abilities and skills to pull us out of the mess). It is interesting to see how these dominant attitudes have appropriated a show of the intellectual virtues, a large repertoire, with variants for each step of the social ladder. But the brightest show of mental alertness, and the heaviest show of moral righteousness (lightened by the much-admired inflection of irony) cannot conceal the fact that they are, in their fruits, negative, and are at bottom mechanical: the reflexes of a mass-hypnosis. Mass hypnosis is no doubt just one aspect of the unity of society, but in our case the mass-hypnosis is negative, so all the particles are negative. A mass-hypnosis can just as well be positive (the turn of the fifteenth/sixteenth centuries in England was certainly mass-hypnotized, but positively). In our case however, each one of us as a microcosm of our society, is afflicted with the negative sleep, in some degree or other, whether we like it or not, and each one of us has to struggle separately to become aware of it, and to awaken from it, in our own lives.

It was a strong sense of this web of our inertia that made me so sure about just what opposition John Moat's experiment would meet: opposition from the sources of the cash it would need, from the Educational Institutions that would have to cooperate to supply most of the students, and even from the students themselves.

These expectations of mine were sharply modified at my very next encounter with him. He had invited me to read verse to the students of that first course, on their last evening. And there for the first time I met what has since become familiar, the indescribable, strange, intense euphoria of a successful Arvon course. By the time I had looked through what these students had written in the previous five days, I was converted. Something extraordinary had happened. Somehow John Fairfax and John Moat had hit on a method that actually worked. The deep lanes of mid-Devon cast a dark, narrow shadow, but the voltage of new-found imagination and eloquence and originality in these students' pages seemed like an explosion. I was taken by surprise and found myself immensely moved and excited.

It seemed to me that what had happened here was more intense than anything of the kind I had witnessed in the United States. It's an impression that has been often confirmed since, because, as is well known, that was only the first course of many. Arvon grew, till now it holds thirty courses a year in the Yorkshire Centre at Lumb Bank and thirty at the original Centre at Totleigh Barton in Devon, and over the years it has employed hundreds of writers as tutors. Evidently my feelings about the English temperament had overlooked something. That temperament — if such a common characteristic can be said to exist, without our terms being so general as to be meaningless — is apparently wonderfully well suited to Arvon. But then, maybe the American 'temperament' would respond to it just as intensely and passionately — and the Italian and the Chinese too for that matter — because it would be a new thing to all of them. The five day top-pressure, all-out concentration on producing, with writers and students, as masters and apprentices, living together, secluded from all outside interference, even doing their own cooking, is as far as I know unique to Arvon.

And even if I am largely right about our prevailing mass-hypnosis (and published statistics say I am, they say we think we are on the whole in a phase of self-doubt and negative withdrawal, even if there were no other evidence), nevertheless the Arvon method has evidently hit on the precise formula, the perfect Open Sesame needed to crack that shell of imposed National passivity-to-entropy, that simian laissez-faire, and release the original energy, the hidden creative energy, which is positive.

Still, we always have to answer the Questionner who sits so sly.

And he asks: So let us admit it is as you say, the Arvon Course has this startling effect on the student for a few days, and he or she writes a page that astonishes him or her, and delights the tutors — but what then? Does the whole Machinery of Arvon really come down to this: the student gazing in baffled joy at a few lines of writing, captured from that abnormal, euphoric few days — before it drops him back into the jaws of the world to be chewed up by the forces that chew up the rest of us?

The answer is: Yes it does.

There is much more to that brief answer than might appear. It is too easy to underestimate the import of those few lines and that baffled joy. The moment has to be held under a microscope, and examined carefully. What exactly does happen there? It is too easy to dismiss it as an ephemeral event — an irrelevant and somewhat pathetic pause in the giant struggle of education towards responsibility and citizenship.

To feel the real significance of that seemingly miniature happening, we have to acknowledge what is perhaps not much acknowledged — that far-reaching inner changes, creative revelations of our inner self, the only part of us with any value, are usually triggered in the smallest fraction of time. The operations of the inner life are more analogous to microbiology than to the building of a motorway. Inevitably our lives are shaped by our daily work, but what transforms our innermost self — when it is transformed — are those momentary confrontations, either with some experience that somehow opens internal connections between unexplored parts of ourselves, or with some person whose mere presence, the mere example of their living being, does the same, or with some few seconds of spontaneous vision that does the same. The analogy is with contracting an infection — the single touch of the virus is enough, only in this case what spreads through the cells is illumination, a new richness of life, a deeper grip on ourselves.

And this does happen on the Arvon courses. It cannot be measured, but we have the evidence of those students who describe an experience which can only be this, in some degree or other. And they are now very many.

Even so, it may be that the persistent Questionner will go on. Is that enough? he will ask. That hit or miss chance of starting somebody off on a new feeling about themselves, which might be illusory, which might lead them to dream up unreal futures for themselves, doomed to disappointment, which might even — horror! — fix them in a determination to become writers. Is that what Arvon is about? Do we really want more writers?

There is no arguing with one who lowers the meaning of everything by simply lowering the interpretation, and who distrusts all that is invisible and intangible. For one thing, he has all the hard evidence on his side, even when he goes on to tell us that man is a political animal, a machine only, and that all culture is an opiate, a temporary illusion, and that our inner lives are a vapour — of no more account or reality than the inner lives of slaughter-house sheep.

But by then we know we have to dismiss this Questionner, much as we respect his point of view. It is better, perhaps, not to let him get his teeth into the fact that those who have taken part in the stirring events of a good Arvon course are also sometimes troubled.

This troubled feeling is intimately blended with the exhilaration. It is a feeling somewhat akin to the near-despair a teacher sometimes feels — I have certainly felt it — confronting a classful of very bright eleven-year-olds. What sort of teaching can ever hope to take advantage of all that eager potential, all that joyful readiness to go to the limit?

When the Arvon student is put in possession of that creative self, which was hitherto inaccessible, two things, in particular, suddenly become much more interesting: the working of language, and the use of literature. In other words, that event brings about, often in a very short time, but in an organic and natural way, what years of orthodox English teaching almost inevitably fail to bring about, except in the most artificial and external way. The student is awakened to the real life of language, with all that implies of the physiology of words, their ancestry and history and dynamic behaviour in varying circumstances (of all abbreviated, in conventional teaching, under the heading: grammar). At the same time he is introduced to literature as a living organism, part of the human organism, something which embodies the psychological record of this drama of being alive, something which articulates and illuminates the depth and range and subtlety of being human. Literature becomes as personal to him as his own struggling abilities — no longer, as conventional teaching presents it (and can only present it), a museum of obsolete manners and dead artefacts, without any relevance to 'now and the future'.

And in all this, the student has not swallowed anything from outside. It has all been awakened inside. In the true sense of the word he has been 'educated'.

But this is not all. While this is happening, maybe the largest purpose of all is being achieved. Our best imaginative literature can well be called the sacred book of the tribe. It holds what we, as a tribe, have inwardly — and therefore with most decisive experience — lived through: it holds the inner vision we all share, the unbroken circle of our nationality. This living monument of our language is the closest thing we have to a mythology: it is sacred because it enshrines our deepest knowledge of ourselves as a people, the language-circuits of our thought and feeling. It holds the D.N.A. of our consciousness as a spiritual unity. The literature and the language are one. And we value it for the same reason that all nations in good morale have valued their literature: it is the national soul we carry. And our intimate possession of it, and our attempt to relive and renew and develop its traditions in our own lives is what keeps us single and alive as a nation. And when a student has been awakened, as I have described, to language and literature, he has been initiated into custodianship of this sacred book, the coherence of Englishness. And if this is not important, I do not know what is. After all, it is very easy to let that inner coherence go. It is easy to reject or neglect our sacred book: all sorts of novelties can persuade a people to do that, and laziness, more surely than an invader's imposed law, can easily obliterate our continually renewed efforts to bind ourselves into it afresh. It is very easy for a nation to break up into fragments and die. It has often happened. And that misfortune is something that cannot be rationalized away.

So what is troubling about the success of the Arvon method is in that very success, the sight of these truly basic educational activities being so joyously grasped by the students — but for how long?

Any hope we might have for their survival, once the five days are over, must be qualified by what we know of the survival rate of natural talent, in contemporary England. One of the most suggestive arguments is to be found in the Anthologies which have been published, for the last twenty-three years, by the annual Children's Literary Competition, run by W. H. Smith (it was formerly run by the *Daily Mirror*). In this Competition, between thirty thousand and sixty thousand entries are judged every year, from children all over the UK, in different age-groups between eight and seventeen years-old. Each year, the judges of that Competition confront a display of natural verbal and imaginative gifts that could not easily be richer: what might be called maximum talent in this field seems to be not at all uncommon. But after twenty-three years, the judges are forced to ask: what has happened to them all? The impression is: they disappeared into some disintegrating gas, around the age of eighteen. Because almost without exception they have disappeared.

The judges are forced to ask, too, whether the same nearly total wipe-out occurs in every other field, where the talent is less naturally visible, and the productions are not measured in such open National Competitions.

The Social epidemic, whatever it is, that swallows these, also waits for Arvon's students. We can accuse fashionable culture, which is certainly inimical to the nurture of language, and we can take the measure of that strange hostility to literature — to the written word in any form — which has even managed to acquire political status, and even a role in education — with an ideology and a revolutionary educational programme. And we can wonder about the tolerance where such hostility is called everything but high treason of a most effective sort. But these, after all, are only symptoms.

Which returns us forcibly to the motives behind this present book.

During the twelve years of its existence, Arvon has exposed a large number of writers to the problems of being a course tutor. This steady effort of exploration and discovery, in the actual methods of working with apprentice writers, has accumulated gradually, as the tutors have returned again and again, sharing the work with fresh partners. It is this battery of experience which John Moat and John Fairfax have been able to tap. They have tutored regularly themselves, from that first course onwards, and as the originators of the whole idea they have come to feel, perhaps more acutely than anybody else, that the technical part of the work, at least, is something that ought to be shared more widely — among teachers, it may be, who have never heard of Arvon, and among students who will never get there.

Whatever happens on these courses — and as I have tried to indicate much of what happens can be momentous in a psychological way — the actual hour-by-hour work is mainly a business of scrutinizing language in action, a laborious business of discrimination and definition, fitting words to one precise purpose or another.

And this is an activity which can be exercised anywhere, in a classroom or in private. It does not need the special circumstances of an Arvon course to justify its usefulness.

If we were a healthy society, presumably we would not need to be schooled so deliberately into an understanding of the life of our own language — our society itself would supply the understanding naturally and fully, in the flourishing use of our mother-tongue. But we have to admit our society fails there. Even such a minimal cultural essential as respect for literacy, and for the worlds of meaning that open within words, even so much as could be taken for granted in a nineteenth century Lancashire weaver, or a Welsh collier of fifty years ago, or a Scots shepherd, cannot any longer be left for our society to provide of itself, by its own initiative. It seems to me we now have to regard the body of our language as we might regard the deprived body of a man in prison: only a deliberate regimen of planned exercise will keep it going at all, let alone develop athletic prowess. Language is not so natural, even among such higher primates as we are. Whatever else we forget we should not forget that a man, deprived of all stimulation for about five days, forgets language.

Arvon has been a very conscious response to the crisis we have been talking about. And this book is an attempt to spread the response further, into schools and into the public at large, by the two men who first put Arvon together, and who have already given much of their lives to it.

Chapter One

AIMS AND BEGINNINGS

Can One be Taught to Write Well?

The misconception that professional writers encounter more often than any other is that their art is something that cannot be taught. But all art is achieved through the exercise of a craft, and every craft has its rudiments that must be taught. The craft of writing is no exception.

Sir Ernest Gowers ends his prologue to his magnificent manual of usage with these words:

> Let us therefore agree, before we go any further, that a reasonably good standard of writing is a mark not of preciosity but of good sense, not of prissiness but of efficiency; that such a standard can be attained by anyone with a little effort; that the effort will be worthwhile . . . ; that it requires neither hairsplitting nor self-consciousness but merely a willingness to acquire good habits; and, finally, that a writer with good habits may be allowed to make an occasional slip, just as a good doctor or lawyer may occasionally give the wrong advice or a good cashier the wrong change, without incurring eternal damnation.

Here Sir Ernest refers to the *general* craft of writing. There are, of course, many specialist crafts within the spectrum of writing: poetry, journalism, writing for television and so forth (for which, it is planned, this series will provide manuals at a later date). In other words every writer finds that his work is governed not only by the general craft, but also by its own specialist craft. And it is with the general craft of creative or imaginative writing that this book is concerned.

There have been many books that have attempted to throw light on this facet of the craft, and mostly they have been scholarly, detailed and intensely demanding. Experience from working for twelve years with almost every conceivable category of student has convinced us that there is a demand for a book that is simple and practical, useful equally to the beginner, to someone, not necessarily

1

a beginner, who is called on to teach elementary creative writing and feels the need for a guide, and for someone who is working on his or her own. It is to meet precisely this need that this short book has been written.

What Can/Cannot be Learned from a Book?

What we write must, of course, be our own. This means that however much or little we can be taught about *how* to write, we cannot become writers solely by learning. To be a writer one has got to be gifted.

But having said that, it should be added very quickly that the gift for writing, enough to make the pursuit meaningful and a source of pleasure, is much more common than many suppose. Talent isn't found exclusively in the sixth form or the university English Department but, to judge from our experience, just as probably in a glove-factory or farmers' co-op, among businessmen or housewives.

> If you wish to be a good writer, write.
>
> Epictetus

The gift to write is a wind that blows where it lists.
What then is left to be learned? It can be put in three categories.

1. What can be learned from a book
2. What can be learned only by writing
3. What can be learned only from a teacher

Before going further it is important to be clear about these three categories.

The Book

Most beginners, when they contemplate a piece of work they have finished, usually experience a vague sense of satisfaction, and a vague sense of dissatisfaction. But above all they feel helpless — no idea how to make the meaning clearer, or the impact stronger; no idea how to improve the writing. They don't know whether what they have written is good or bad; and they don't know because they have never been taught.

A person who continues to write in this uncertainty is denied perhaps the only genuine satisfaction that writing has to offer: the excitement of *worrying* one's work, of bringing craft to bear so that the writing achieves maximum precision and effect.

A book can make this possible. It won't get you to the end of the corridor, but it can open the door and set you on your way.

A book can present general guidelines, and these are precious to the beginner, and useful to the more practised writer. They include pointers to the effective choice of language, to the relative strength of various parts of speech and figures of speech, demonstrations of effective use of syntax. These guidelines are elemental rather than elementary; and this means that their relevance is something we never outgrow.

The Work

It is only by working, by writing, by practising the art long and regularly that a writer develops his ear, i.e. that sense which eventually enables a writer to *hear* where the power of the word lies and, ultimately, his own voice.

What is meant by a writer's voice? His individual use of language which enables him at last to come at the material which only he can express. It is the hallmark of the accomplished writer and his or her unique *authority*.

The Teacher

For every writer there must come a time when the general grounding is no longer reliable, when he must look for guidance beyond the book. At this point the only reliable guide is someone who has travelled further along the way. In other words, a practitioner of the art, someone who has made the pursuit of writing his life or her life. In one word, a writer.

How does one go about finding such a teacher? In England it has at least become easier over the last twelve years. Since 1969 The Arvon Foundation*, with the support of, at the latest count, some three hundred and fifty writers, has established an enterprise which

---

*The Arvon Foundation: Totleigh Barton, Sheepwash, Beaworthy, Devon EX21 5N6
Lumb Bank, Hebden Bridge, West Yorkshire HX7 6DF.

3

makes such encounters possible. Which, in other words, provides

> Probably, indeed, the larger part of the labour of an author in composing his work is critical labour: the labour of sifting, combining, constructing, expunging, correcting, testing: this frightful toil is as much critical as creative.
>
> T. S. Eliot

inexperienced writers with the opportunity of working in conducive circumstances with professional writers, specialists in many of the craft's various disciplines (from poetry to writing for radio, from T.V. scripts to writing for children).

The form of training that this enterprise provides is essential to every student of writing, and so must inevitably be related to that offered in this book. And the more ostensibly so since much of the material that follows, and the selection of the bulk of the exercises, have been derived from the authors' twelve years' experience at Arvon with students of just about every conceivable age and background.

Departures and Destinations

'I feel I would like to write, but I've no idea where or how to begin.'

For a start, stop looking over your shoulder.

One qualification, only one, is required. The desire to write. If you desire to write you can gratify that desire only by writing. Words? Yes, you'll need a few. What you will not need is an academic qualification, or anybody else's material.

The desire to write is the need to express *oneself* in writing. So first one has to be oneself. And next, if one's writing is to be in any way reliable, one must be true to oneself. No emulating what others

> To speak of one's emotions without fear or moral ambition, to come out from under the shadow of other men's minds, to forget their needs, to be utterly oneself, that is all the Muses care for.
>
> W. B. Yeats

are up to. This may sound all too simple, too simple even to constitute a challenge. Believe that and you delude yourself. It is, as any writer will confess and show scars to prove, a challenge sufficient to demand not less than everything, and no less than a lifetime.

To begin to write one must begin to write. And to do that one needs equipment, and one needs time, and ideally (at least most of us find) one needs space.

Equipment

Pencil and paper? It is true, that will suffice — at a pinch. But you will be better equipped if you have also a typewriter and a dictionary. Any old typewriter but the best dictionary you can lay hands on.

A typewriter is useful for two reasons. First, if one intends to submit work for publication, anything that makes the manuscript easy to read is useful. Editors recoil from handwritten manuscripts. Second, it is very difficult to view objectively a piece of work in one's own handwriting but the clean edge of type detaches the eye and one can view one's writing more dispassionately. One can see much more easily what is wrong, and much more readily take it to task.

The dictionary. Simply, for the journeyman writer it is the carpetbag that carries his stock-in-trade: words.

One might mention others: Thesauruses, Word-finders, Rhyming-dictionaries. Optional gear. They have their uses, but most often they are misused. When they become labour-savers they are deadly. Shakespeare got by without any of them. It's even on record that he didn't use a typewriter.

Time

'I would love to write, but I just cannot make the time.'

In every manual on virtually any discipline from meditation to golf, stress is laid on the necessity for regular practice. Writing is no exception. 'Never a day without a line' isn't an idle precept. Any writer will tell how the more regularly he writes the more readily the words present themselves — and how difficult it is to get back to work after even a short break. As the years pass it becomes only more difficult. The machine is lubricated by regular use.

The kindest advice to the beginner is, Write Every Day. As little as half-an-hour, it doesn't much matter how little. And it doesn't much matter what. If you're stuck with your novel or you're out of ideas, then go back to the journal or start writing down your dreams. Write regularly and you'll be amazed how soon the mind gets the hang of it. It will take up and leave off without fuss and that time will establish itself the writing time.

Claim that time to yourself. Claim it against the clamouring of all the world, and soon the world, even friends, even parents, even children, will come to respect it.

Space

Most writers find it useful to have one place which is either set aside for their work or, if that is not possible, which they can use when they are working. If not a room, or a hut, or an attic, then a part of a room — or even just a particular chair. The place then becomes associated with work. As soon as one goes there the mind knows what is expected of it and it settles to work.

In all narration there is only one way to be clever. And that is to be exact.

Robert Louis Stevenson

Methods of Work

The blank page — there are precious few whom it fails to daunt. Looking at it one realizes that here is no life for a person who cringes from making decisions.

In the course of the book we suggest exercises that will help to prime the flow. But what about preparations and ways of working? The answer is that they are various as writers are various.

Some, before they start new work, go on a fast. Some go on a blind. Some just hang around until boredom becomes so unendurable that even work offers a break. Some write compulsively, almost all the time.

Writers have worked in banks, in zoos. Some cannot write to a deadline. Some only when the deadline is past. Some compose as they walk along. Some have written their best work in the trenches. Some have gone to sea to escape the business only to find themselves landed with a Moby Dick.

There's certainly a book to be written on methods of work, but this isn't it. All we will say on the subject is that there are no generalizations save only this one: writing is hard work — hard mentally and psychologically and, for some reason, physically.

When we know how we work best we will have made an important discovery. For a writer that is the best equipment. But we won't find out shivering here on the brink. The plunge then!

Suggested Exercise

The Journal and the Commonplace Book

Consider keeping one or other of these. They make painless the priceless discipline of regular writing. And each in its way becomes a memory to you, a storehouse of material, and a growing delight.

The Journal becomes the daily (or less frequent) record of your life, and in particular the logbook of imaginative or vital experience. It calls on the writer to be constantly alive, alert to the phenomenon of his life. And since he can have no material other than his experience, it serves actually to acquaint him with and define to him his material. The writing in the journal is almost necessarily spontaneous and uncontrived and so near to the heart (which is precisely why the great journals, Dorothy Wordsworth's or Gerard Manley Hopkins's, are so precious); and for this reason a writer will very often in his journal discover his own voice.

The Commonplace Book can be all that a journal is, but will include another element. Into it goes any phrase overheard or read, any passage of writing or pilferable image — anything that has moved or startled or impressed the mind or heart. So the whole becomes a precious jackdaw hoard to which one can refer and upon which one can draw. Date the entries and you will find over the years it becomes an extraordinary record of one's imaginative development.

It serves another vital purpose. By actually writing down the fined expression of thought or fine description of accomplished writers, one experiences the means, the grain of cadence, the drama of syntax much more immediately than by mere reading. By this means one is informed of the mastery of craft.

Chapter Two

WORDS: A DEMONSTRATION OF POWER

In the beginning was the word . . .

If we are to believe the Bible, it was by uttering nouns, or names, that God created: 'And God said, Let there be light: and there was light.' We can argue as to whether God had already conceived this light in His mind. But clearly it wasn't until He uttered the word that light came into being.

Words, then, are powerful.

The Explosive Word

How can the power of words be demonstrated? Most people are familiar with the pop psychoanalyst's game of word-response. Imagine this employed by a teacher. A teacher says to his students: 'In a second I'll ask you to close your eyes. When you do, notice how suddenly you are on your own, isolated within the silence or the backchat of your own head. Concentrate on that. Right, now close your eyes, and listen.'

The students close their eyes. The room is still.

The teacher continues: 'In a minute I shall utter one single word. Listen carefully for it. Let it explode in the black silence of your brain. The instant you hear it, open your eyes and write down on a scrap of paper the *one single word* which is called into your mind in response to the word I have spoken. For instance, I might call 'BIRD'. And if so you might find you came up with SONG or DUCK or CHICK or BATH or CYNTHIA or something else. Simple. Are you ready? Now listen.'

The students listen.

'RED,' says the teacher.

Instantly the eyes open, and pens respond.

In turn, the students read out their words: LETTERBOX, FIRE, FURY, BLOOD, FLAMING, BLOODY, BULL, COMMUNIST,

OUCH! BLOOD, JUMPER, ROSE, SUNSET, RACHEL, BOOK, HORRIBLE.
One word says so much! The power let loose is astonishing. Then the discussion begins.
How many words appear more than once? Two bloods and a bloody, otherwise all different. Presumably if the teacher had asked for two words in response there'd have been no two responses the same. What can be inferred from this? In no time these conclusions will have been reached:

1. That words *are* powerful. They have power to evoke a response.
2. That the response is not standard, but would appear to be influenced by *individuality* and by *circumstance*.
3. That therefore if a writer is to evoke the response he desires he'll need to be very careful and very skilful.

> When we can take the green from grass, blue from heaven, and red from blood, we have already an enchanter's power — upon one plane; and the desire to wield that power in the world external to our minds awakes. It does not follow that we shall use that power well on any plane. We may put a deadly green upon a man's face and produce horror; we may make the rare and terrible blue moon to shine; or we may cause weeds to spring with silver leaves and rams to wear fleeces of gold, and put hot fire in the belly of the cold worm.
>
> J. R. R. Tolkien

Individuality and Circumstance

Read these two extracts and feel how different in each case is the response to the word *Poppy*:

> Mad Patsy said, he said to me,
> That every morning he could see
> An angel walking on the sky;
> Across the sunny skies of morn
> He threw great handfuls far and nigh
> Of poppy seed among the corn;
> And then, he said, the angels run
> To see the poppies in the sun.
> James Stephens

9

and,

> In Flanders fields the poppies blow
> Between the crosses, row on row . . .

The same word. The same flower. But what worlds apart.

Individuality

Two people are reading the same story, *The Little Prince*. One requires a box of man-size tissues to cope with the tears. The other snarls, 'Eyewash', and tosses the book into the coal-scuttle. Two people read in the paper a report of a bomb-throwing incident. One goes to the cupboard, takes down a box of grenades, and hurries out of the house without shutting the door. The other puts the page aside for his next double portion of chips.

Circumstance

A four-letter word in the changing-room after a hard match lost on a disputed penalty in the third minute of injury time — it will barely ripple the surface of the communal tub. But that same word, shouted above the small talk at the Lord Mayor's Banquet . . .

So words *are* explosive. *But* the extent of the explosion will differ according to the individual and the circumstance.

The Sorcerer

Nowadays we take words so much for granted, so much as our birthright, that we've ceased to question or wonder at their power. This, though, has not always been the case. Once men were very aware that words were so powerful that they could (with knowledge) be used to achieve virtually anything. To summon a spirit to produce a rainshower out of a clear sky.

The sorcerer (call him what you will — alchemist, magician, wizard) realized that of all mysteries the most demonstrable, and the one with the most bearing on existence, meaning and power, is that there are *no two things under the sun the same*. No two pebbles on the beach, no two leaves in the forest. No two human beings. The sorcerer knew that each individual, simply because each *is* individual, has his or her or its own name. Not a generic name, not a random surname . . . but the mysterious magical name that is the expression of this unique identity.

In the myth ('Myth, the popular expression of man's deepest knowledge') the creator utters the name, and it is this naming that actually calls the creature (i.e. that which is created) into existence.

It is the same with us and our thoughts. Can you imagine a thought in your mind before it has come into words? Can it *exist* without words? Or put it this way. You come across an object and you don't know what it is. But then suddenly you see. Your mind tells you, 'Oh, it's a jam-jar!' With your naming of it, the object, for you, comes into being.

'In the beginning was the word . . .' Precisely.

The Art of Calling Things Names

It was because the sorcerer knew about the power of names that he understood why he should take such care of his own name. Let another get hold of your name and he could put you in a bottle.

> Unable to discriminate clearly between words and things, the savage commonly fancies that the link between a name and the person or things denominated by it is not merely arbitrary and ideal association, but a real and substantial bond which unites the two in such a way that magic may be wrought on a man just as easily through his name as through his hair, his nails, or any other material part of his person. In fact, primitive man regards his name as a vital portion of himself and takes care of it accordingly.
> Sir James G. Frazer

The name must be kept from enemies, and given only as the ultimate sign of love and trust.

Look at these three lines from a student's poem to a friend.

> Paul Hoskins
> Seen walking the streets at midnight
> Thinking too deeply.

That's quite alarming. What right had he to tell us so much about his friend?

Names — we tend to overlook their power. But we do still acknowledge their significance in many ways. For instance in the Christian wedding ceremony. To seal the marriage, the woman takes the man's name. There could be no more complete a way of signifying that the two are made one. A binding spell.

The secret is the name. Names are words. So words are dangerous.

Perhaps now the definition: 'POETRY IS THE ART OF CALLING THINGS NAMES', will not sound so flippant. If calling things names *is* creating, then this definition implies all that is serious about the writer's calling. The honesty, the responsibility, and the danger. Get the name, the spell, wrong, and you may create something the world will regret.

Look at this extraordinary poem, written by a boy of sixteen. An astonishing gift of self-definition, and self-denial. An amazing use of name.

ON THE FLIP SIDE IS ME

Nobody looks at me,
Or wonders who I am.
Insignificantly, I sit and contemplate
What fame and fortune would mean to me.
When I die there will be no statue,
No television programme or thousands of pop records —
Just a lot of earth
And perhaps a gravestone.

I would like to be remembered
As the weird from Littleham,
Who supported the mini-skirt,
The see-through blouse;
Who spoke up for young Jimi amongst the crowd;
Who laughed at such phrases as
'Marmalade skies', 'Tangerine trees',
'Semolina Pilchard climbing the Eiffel Tower';
As the weird who wrote poems
And was always talking about Bramha;
Who had the words of the month such as:
Euphoric, Narcissus, Eros, Rump, Erotic;
As the weird behind all new trendy trends such as:
Pink and yellow striped underwear,
And broken duffle-coats.

But if I am remembered,
I will be remembered as:
The outcast,

Who answers to Flash,
And owns the sad, sad name of Steven Leonard Flather.

What does this spell achieve? He gives away his secret. He is now no longer alone.

Everyday Magic

Words are magical. And using words, all of us, every day, we are magicians. We are all constantly casting spells.

Imagine this:

A number of people are having a meal. You are at one end of the table. The bread is at the other. There's a guy called John sitting in the middle. And you want the bread.

Almost without thinking, you say: 'John, please will you pass the bread.' Almost without thinking John passes the bread.

Now imagine there is someone sitting at the table who has no words — he isn't deaf, but just somehow has never come across words, or heard spoken language. Why should he be amazed, so utterly aghast? He hears you make some extraordinary sounds. He sees, clearly in response, one person, a particular person, look up and do what you want, *perform your will.* It is magic. It has to be.

And what you have done, and take so much for granted, is in fact very subtle and very precious. First, you have summoned a particular person by name. Then you have employed a charm, the word *please.* In this way you have not ordered, but *bound* the person. With this one amazing word, which expresses obligation, respect and dependence, you have made your request both acceptable and difficult to deny. And then you have named the bread.

He passes the bread. You've successfully cast your spell.

You might have said, 'Bread, please!' That would have been another spell. But being less precise it might not have worked.

You might have yelled, 'Belt up and pass the bread!' Very powerful. You'd have got a response all right, and probably the bread too, in your face. You'd have got the spell wrong.

But no, you command the subtle magic. You offend no one. You get what you want.

Bread — The Levels of Meaning

Concentrate on the word *bread.* According to the dictionary: 'bread is an article of food prepared by moistening, kneading, and baking meal or flour, usually with the addition of yeast or leaven.'

Does that cover everything? Perhaps not the loaf once advertised in the USA as specially designed to reassume perfect shape after being entirely crushed in your shopping bag.

And the Luddite when he saw the silicone chip, does the dictionary cover his use of the word; 'That one will have my bread and butter.'?

Or if we pray, 'Give us this day our daily bread'? Surely the dictionary barely touches on this meaning; this bread is a different sustenance, more akin to manna. Or to grace.

Or what the pusher said in a novel, does it cover his use: 'You want some tea, man? Then put your bread where your mouth is!'?

And if in our time we find the staple word bread has come to mean money, then perhaps words are yet more telling than we had supposed.

We saw at the beginning how words mean different things to different people in different circumstances. Now we see that words in themselves carry different levels of meaning. Or since we are also talking about power, it would be more accurate to say that they are *charged* with different levels of meaning.

Is it, then, possible to find a setting or order for words which imply in a single statement more than one level of meaning? If it were possible, would not that statement be doubly powerful?

A poem necessarily is one such statement.

THIS BREAD I BREAK

This bread I break was once the oat,
This wine upon a foreign tree
Plunged in its fruit;
Man in the day or wind at night
Laid the crops low, broke the grape's joy.

Once in the wind the summer blood
Knocked in the flesh that decked the vine,
Once in this bread
The oat was merry in the wind;
Man broke the sun, pulled the wind down.

This flesh you break, this blood you let
Make desolation in the vein,
Were oat and grape
Born of the sensual root and sap;
My wine you drink, my bread you snap.

Dylan Thomas

The Exploration of Truth

The man who writes instructions for opening a jam-jar presumably aims to employ just the one clear level of meaning. Obviously he must tell the truth, but the job shouldn't be too difficult. (Though you may remember the famous, 'Pierce with pin and push off.' After all, it isn't *that* easy.)

The man who writes the advertisements — he is more concerned with response than truth. But however we rate his intentions we can't deny his power to cast spells. After all, if you come home with the right tin, it is a Heinz souper-day. For Heinz at any rate. So in a sense he too tells the truth.

What about the scientist? He is concerned with the truth, the laws and generalities of the universe. But when did laws and generalities ever describe a single individual. Are individuals untrue? The scientist then is concerned with just the one facet of truth.

A good journalist is concerned with truth — with the facts, with what one might call the representation of human history as it happens. But is this truth? You read two good journalists' reports of the same incident, and they are different. Can they *both* be the truth? If so, what is truth?

What then of the creative writer (by which we mean the imaginative writer and the poet)? His service to truth is not that he write *about* it, or make records of it, or employ it, or promote it, but that he

---

Art makes and unmakes many worlds, and can draw the moon from heaven by a silver thread. Hers are the forms 'more real than living men', and hers the great archetypes of which things that have existence are but unfinished copies. Nature has, in her eyes, no laws, no uniformity. She can work miracles at her will, and when she calls monsters from the deep they come. She can bid the almond tree blossom in the winter, and send snow upon the ripe cornfield.

Oscar Wilde

It is a strange truth: that your poem 'Counter-Attack' frightened me more than the real one: though the boy at my side, shot through the head, lay on top of me, soaking my shoulder, for half an hour.

Wilfred Owen

amplify truth by celebrating it. Dylan Thomas wrote:

'A good poem is a contribution to reality. The world is never the same once a good poem has been added to it. A good poem helps to change the shape and significance of the universe, helps to extend everyone's knowledge of himself and the world around him . . .'

In sum, then, such a writer is concerned with a kind of magic — that which uses words to call new things into being. The pronouncement of new names. And such writing is an art which, like every other art, requires imagination, a willingness to learn the craft and a great deal, perhaps a lifetime, of practice. But which, most important, and unlike any other art, requires the command of words.

Suggestions for Practice

Read again Dylan Thomas' 'This Bread I Break'. Consider the different levels of meaning.

Compose a sentence or a number of sentences in which the nouns (names) are changed with more than one level of meaning.

16

Chapter Three

THE FIVE SENSES

We are told that when Jesus was crucified he suffered five wounds. One on each hand and foot where it was nailed, and the one in his side where he was pierced by the soldier's spear. This fact is included in many accounts and legends, and always the Five Wounds are treated as having special significance. But in one legend Christ's wounds signify man's five senses: Touch, Sight, Hearing, Scent and Taste. Here the suggestion is that in man the spirit (i.e. Christ) is nailed by the five senses to the physical body (i.e. the Cross).

Presumably this legend came into being when someone observed that all information about the external, tangible world is fed into man by way of one or more of his five senses. Or put another way, it is by our senses that we are alive to, and so in a sense joined to, and so in a sense nailed to our physical or material surroundings.

What this says about the senses is worth noting — that they are dangerous, at times even cruel but, certainly for the artist, also of priceless value.

Pick up some small object in the fingers of one hand. Watch, more intently than you have ever watched before, as your fingers feel and discover for you the nature of that object. The smoothness or roughness. Each little scar in the surface. Whether it is damp or dry. Whether it is soft, heavy, warm or cold. Look at the astonishing design of those fingers, how they move, and the sensitivity with which they feel. Try to imagine, or even to picture, how all that they discover is transmitted, presumably up your arm, to the 'reception centre' somewhere behind your eyes.

> Art bids us touch and taste and hear and see the world, and shrinks from what Blake calls mathematical form, from every abstract thing, from all that is of the brain only, from all that is not a fountain jetting from the entire hopes, memories, and sensations of the body.
>
> W. B. Yeats

Then close your eyes. Concentrate on what your fingers, by their touch, tell you about the object.

Most of us remember how as a child we went into an old building, and how in a sudden moment of quiet we heard it whispering, and how we felt that if only we could listen keenly enough we would hear it telling us of everything that had ever happened within its walls, of its entire history. After such an experience it is no great surprise to learn that there are people known as psychometers who have a gift of touch so developed that when they hold an object its whole life — its birth and history, even the landscape and incidents that have surrounded it — is suddenly revealed to them. Hold an object in this way, *sense* it wonderingly, fully, exhaustively, and one will be never quite the same person again. In that moment, reborn to the senses, one realizes that no matter how long one lives one will never get to the end of exploring the mystery of the tangible world.

If there is any sense of anything, then everything is remarkable.

As a writer, your first discipline is *to be alive to* everything. And that means that here and now you begin to exercise and sharpen your five senses: Touch, Sight, Hearing, Scent and Taste.

Words and the Five Senses

Explore how the five senses make you alive not only to your surroundings, but also to words. Take the word *cow*.

A boy has lived all his life in the town. For him *cow* is a creature with horns which someone keeps at a safe distance somewhere round the back of that slot-machine in the High Street that's filled with cardboard cartons of milk.

The boy goes on a train journey. Now for him *cow* is that creature he saw, red in the sunlight, half as big as a bus, bolting nimble as a kitten, and with its tail crooked in a question mark over its back, away from the rush of the train (probably a bullock — cows don't give a damn about trains).

The boy spends Easter on a farm. Now for him *cow* is as follows:

1. A long drooling tongue that pulls at his fingers, and scrapes like No. 4 sandpaper.
2. The fine steam rising in the first warm sunlight over thirty, broad glistening backs. Seven o'clock in the morning.
3. The sound the other side of the tall hedge, the scrunch, scrunch, scrunch of the chewed cud. Oh, and then late at night the terrible bellow of one who's had her calf taken away.
4. The warm secret smell of the cowshed — the new milk, the straw, the dung, and the great living sides of beef.

5. The day the herd gets back in the new pasture, after winter-feeding, and for the first time the milk tastes green.

That's five — the five senses.

> 'He said, "What's time? Leave Now for dogs and apes! Man has For ever".' True, but the works of man, unless they are of 'now' and of 'this place', can have no 'for ever'.
>
> David Jones

Now he's more alive to what a cow is. The truth is he's learning the secret of the name. At last he has some idea of what the word means. When he goes back to town he'll be using a different language. Why, he might even write about a cow.

You see what has happened? He now has authority — over a cow.

The Writer's Chore

Read this:

> Aug. 13 — Heavy seas: we walked along the sea wall to the Kennaway Tunnel to watch them. The wave breaks in this order — the crest of the barrel 'doubling' (that, a boatman said, is the word in use) is broken into a bush of foam, which, if you search it, is a lace and tangle of jumping sprays; then breaking down these grow to a sort of shaggy quilt tumbling up the beach; thirdly this unfolds into a sheet of clear foam and running forward it leaves and laps the wave reaches its greatest height upon the shore and at the same time its greatest clearness and simplicity; after thàt, raking on the shingle and so on, it is forked and torn and, as it commonly has a pitch or lurch to one side besides its backdraught, these rents widen; they spread and mix and the water clears and escapes to the sea transparent and keeping in the end nothing of its white except in long dribble-bubble strings which trace its set and flow.

There you see a writer, one of the finest, at work. The extract is from Gerard Manley Hopkins's Journal. Do you notice how his eye 'does over' the wave exactly as your fingers 'did over' that object? One might say that in each case the eye or the fingers *made the object its own*.

Apart from what the passage says about the wave, there are a number of other things it tells us:

1. That Hopkins was interested in and alive to that wave. Which is why we are interested.
2. That after he'd written this piece exploring the wave, he was 'never the same again'. There was more of him. He was more conscious. The word *wave* now meant this much more to him, and he would use it differently. He had new authority.
3. That, for some reason, he had needed to express what he felt about this wave.
4. That he chose to express what he felt, *not by writing about the feeling,* but by describing as precisely as he was able *the thing he had felt,* i.e. the wave. He re-created the wave.

Now what he might have said, and it would in a sense have been just as true, is: 'The other day I went and had a look at the sea and found it all very interesting.' But what, what precisely, would that have told us, or, more important, him? Precisely nothing, because there is nothing precise, nothing individual. Anyone might have said that any day of the week. In one flash you have seen the difference between literature and reportage. This is something we'll return to, but for the moment see how literature is more exact, more informative, more lively, more *individual,* and a lot more work!

Let's go back a minute to what we discussed in chapter one: to individuality. If Hopkins had looked at a different wave he'd have described it differently. Or if you'd been there and had looked at the same wave, you'd have described it differently. He couldn't possibly have described it as you'd have seen it — because he didn't have your authority.

So then we see that this individual expression is two-way: it describes the object *and* the subject; the wave *and* himself. He is a man who felt *this* about *this* wave. An encounter, in fact.

This is true of all literature. It is the record — and as such the celebration — of an encounter. The subject with the object. Hopkins with his wave. The object may be a thing, as with the wave, or it may be an experience, like falling in love or out of bed. And it may be factual, or it may be imaginary — it makes not a scrap of difference.

In truth great love springs from great knowledge of the beloved object, and if you know it but little you will be able to love it only a little or not at all . . .

Leonardo da Vinci

20

Since subject and object are each individual, so must the exact record of their encounter be individual. And that, from what has already been said, means that the record is unique, and remarkable, and magical.

Stop a second, just think again what it is we have said.

By using his five senses each one of us is constantly creating his own particular universe around him. Each one of us then is the remarkable author of his own remarkable universe. Or he is if:

1. He's true to his individuality.
2. He's alive to his senses.
3. He's curious about his mysterious surroundings.
4. He feels moved to that one discovery which he can make only by *expressing* himself.

A fine writer in discovering his own universe discovers it for us all.

The Discarded Tree

Sometimes it takes a while to convince people that they're more likely to come up with a piece of powerful writing if they describe a small definable *thing* rather than a huge indefinable *feeling*.

A writer was taking a course in writing. As a first exercise he sent his students off on their own to *quicken* their senses, and to make a short description of some object that interested them. After a time one of the students returned and handed him this:

> The limb is unyielding
> It gives nothing,
> Yet it accepts.
> Life is acceptance.
> Unmovable, yet moved by life
> Struggling painfully
> Thrusting, scarred
> Disfigured.
> Beautiful in Acceptance
> Beautiful through acceptance.
> Acceptance is beauty
> The struggle is the
> Outward sign of
> The beauty.

The writer stared into the mist. There was something there. He tried to focus. Suddenly he had an inspiration. 'It's a war-veteran.'

The student shook her head. 'No,' she said. 'It's a tree.'

The writer took a big, silent breath. Where to begin? Then he had an idea. 'Did you make any notes first?'

The girl gave one half of a grimace, which seemed to say, 'Yes, but I wouldn't be showing them to anyone.'

'Please,' he said as if his life depended on it, and then held out his hand. Looking painfully the other way, she parted with them.

'Outside, green. Pink skin shows through. Papery bark, peeling, brown inside. Layer and layer. Crumbly, dirty. Bark crumbles to nothing . . .'

Listen! You can actually hear the time passing as that girl stares out the secret of her tree.

'. . . Ferns and moss around the base, fungi, grass, yellow leaves. Dead leaves. 3 main limbs and one set apart. 2 limbs divide further. Moss feels like a horse's stroke. Small young shoots, fragile, smooth, with a bloom of hairs, minute . . .'

Do you catch it, the living drama, scene by scene, detail by detail, as her exploration continues? And do you notice how much these notes say about her, and her vivid curiosity?

'Leaves, tiny, insignificant except in colouring, barbed, sharp. Filigree against grey-blue sky. Where leaf meets twig, vulnerable.

'Fly sunbathes and cleans his wings, resting on a leaf, cleans legs, spindly. Feels around. He takes off.

'Lean on the tree, unyielding, it gives back hardness. Secure. Unmoving . . .'

And so on.

Not surprisingly, when the girl discarded the piece she thought was her poem, and found instead a shape for her notes, she discovered she had written a poem. She had carved *her* name on *that* tree!

And now read this:

PAIN FOR A DAUGHTER

Blind with love, my daughter
has cried nightly for horses,
those long-necked marchers and churners
that she has mastered, any and all,
reigning them in like a circus hand —
the excitable muscles and the ripe neck;
tending this summer, a pony and foal.
She who is too squeamish to pull
a thorn from the dog's paw,
watched her pony blossom with distemper,

the underside of the jaw swelling
like an enormous grape.
Gritting her teeth with love,
she drained the boil and scoured it
with hydrogen peroxide until pus
ran like milk on the barn floor.

Blind with loss all winter,
in dungarees, a ski jacket and a hard hat,
she visits the neighbors stable,
our acreage not zoned for barns;
they who own the flaming horses
and the swan-whipped thoroughbred
that she tugs at and cajoles,
thinking it will burn like a furnace
under her small-hipped English seat.
Blind with pain she limps home.
The thoroughbred has stood on her foot.
He rested there like a building.
He grew into her foot until they were one.
The marks of the horseshoe printed
into her flesh, the tips of her toes
ripped off like pieces of leather,
three toenails swirled like shells
and left to float in blood in her riding boot.

Blind with fear, she sits on the toilet,
her foot balanced over the washbasin,
her father, hydrogen peroxide in hand,
performing the rites of the cleansing.
She bites on a towel, sucked in breath,
sucked in and arched against the pain,
her eyes glancing off me where
I stand at the door, eyes locked
on the ceiling, eyes of a stranger,
and then she cries . . .
Oh my God, help me!
Where a child would have cried *Mama!*
Where a child would have believed *Mama!*
she bit the towel and called on God
and I saw her life stretch out . . .
I saw her torn in childbirth,
and I saw her, at that moment,
in her own death and I knew that she
knew.

Anne Sexton

'. . . scoured it with hydrogen peroxide . . .', 'The thoroughbred has stood on her foot,' 'Blind with fear, she sits on the toilet . . .'

Is there anyone who would be unable to come up with those lines? Would you have thought those lines poetic enough to appear in a published poem?

But then the writer is not called to express more than his or her *simplest* view of the truth. There it is, living on the page. And we all hurt.

So we have a mother's simple description of her child wounded by a horse. But what does it tell? The mother is watching, and the child does not call out to *her*. But what does it tell? All the winter the child has loved the wild horse — and now it has crushed her foot. But what does it tell? 'Blind with love, my daughter . . .' 'Blind with loss . . .' 'Blind with pain . . .' 'Blind with fear . . .' But, at the end, '. . . she knew.' So what and what does this simple description tell?

That our senses are cruel as nails, but also of priceless value?

Hopkins, saying his piece about the wave, says something about waves, says something about water; something about the sea; about the land; about himself; about . . . Yes, about Him too.

> 'Lord, I pray thee open his eyes that he may see.' And the Lord opened the eyes of the young man; and he saw: and, behold, the mountain was full of horses and chariots of fire.
> Old Testament

'To see eternity in a grain of sand . . .' Precisely. But first you must find, and look at, and *see* that one particular individual grain of sand!

Suggestions for Practice

1. Look up the words author, authority, authentic in a good dictionary and consider how their meanings interrelate.
2. Compose a riddle: five sentences each describing how one of the five senses responds to a single object (as we did in this chapter with *cow*). Don't however mention the object by name: that's the answer to the riddle.
3. Find an object that interests you. Explore it as Hopkins explored his wave. Then write a description to prove the object unique.

Chapter Four

COMPONENTS OF POWER (1)
— Nouns and Verbs

A writer is bound to have some interest in grammar. But his approach to it will not be the same as a grammarian's. A grammarian is a kind of scientist with language, which means he is interested in laws and generalities. But the only interest a writer has in laws is, as we suggested in the first chapter, how they can be individually broken. Or if that's a bit hot, we'll say he's interested in 'the exception that proves the rule' (i.e. every individual). So a writer is interested in grammar only in so far as it can help him to write more effectively.

Here's one example. Presumably at some point everybody has had to learn those definitions for the different parts of speech: 'A noun is a name of a person, place or thing,' and so on. A writer will say, 'If the definition of the parts of speech provides any guideline to the power of words, then I'm interested. It might help me to write more powerfully.'

Let's then see if it does.

Nouns

The word *noun* comes, one way or another, from the Latin word *nomen* which means (here we go again) *a name*. 'The name of a person, place or thing . . .' Knowing what we do about names and the power they command we can surmise that nouns are important. They are, in fact, the most important, and for one good reason. Of all the parts of speech, only nouns are independent. All the rest, directly or by implication, depend on the existence of nouns for their own existence. Nouns depend on nothing.

TIGER. Bang. It stands all on its own.

But, 'RAN' or 'PUNY' or 'INTO' or 'MOREOVER' or 'STEAD-ILY' — they just don't figure. Not on their own.

> Quinquireme of Nineveh from distant Ophir,
> Rowing home to haven in sunny Palestine,
> With a cargo of ivory,
> And apes and peacocks,
> Sandalwood, cedarwood, and cheap white wine.
>   John Masefield
>
>
> And they bought an Owl, and a useful Cart,
> And a pound of Rice, and a Cranberry Tart,
>   And a hive of silvery Bees.
> And they bought a Pig, and some green Jack-daws,
> And a lovely Monkey with lollipop paws,
> And forty bottles of Ring-bo-Ree,
>   And no end of Stilton Cheese . . . .
>   Edward Lear

Nouns, being independent, carry a complete definition. As such, of all words, they have the greatest intensity of meaning. 'Nouns are what any piece of writing is about.' Nouns are, if you like, the heroes. You can expect a writer to take especial care how he chooses his hero.

'. . . Sir, mister, monsieur, herr, senor, don, dom, senhor, signor, sahib, shri, srijut, babu, mirza, tovarich, comrade, citoyen, yeoman, wight, swain, fellow, guy, blade, bloke, beau, chap, cove, card, johnny, gaffer, chappie, goodman . . .'

Fatal to find you'd written about the wrong guy. Or bloke. Because nouns are also the villains.

Concrete and Abstract

We can divide nouns into umpteen categories (in fact as many as there are nouns). But there is one division of important consequence to the writer: the division into *concrete* and *abstract*.

There'll be more to say about the concrete and the abstract when we discuss imagery, but for the moment we should note this. Concrete nouns are those which represent objects, i.e. things that are registered by one or more of our five senses. These then are the names to which we are most receptive; hence they are the writer's most explosive ammunition.

> I tell you; even though like the Sage of sages, you carried in your memory the image of all the beings that peopled the earth or swim in the seas, still all that knowledge would be as nothing for your soul, for all abstract knowledge is a faded reality: this is because to understand the world, knowledge is not enough, you must see it, touch it, live in its presence and drink the vital heat of existence in the very heart of reality . . .
>
> Teilhard de Chardin

An abstract noun, on the other hand, is not strictly the name of a thing at all. Say one aloud, and see if on the dashboard the needles of the five sense-gauges register anything. ETERNITY. No register — not on our gauges. You don't agree? All right, in terms of the five senses, you say what it means. INGRATITUDE. No register. In fact since the meaning of abstract nouns is so vague, a writer often feels bound to act as if they had no meaning at all. As Shakespeare will demonstrate:

'Ingratitude more strong than traitor's arms . . .' In order to give the abstract a meaning he actually measures it out for us . . . with the concrete!

Tell her you are *in love* with her. It sounds grand, but what on earth does it mean? Give her a string of racehorses, or a diamond ring, or a kiss — or just a glance. Then she knows *exactly* what you mean.

THE LOOK

Strephon kissed me in the spring,
　　Robin in the fall,
But Colin only looked at me
　　And never kissed at all.

Strephon's kiss was lost in jest,
　　Robin's lost in play,
But the kiss in Colin's eyes
　　Haunts me night and day.
　　　　　　　　Sara Teasdale

Consider what would have been lost had Sara Teasdale been tempted to stick with look instead of kiss in the second last line. The kiss haunts us too, because it makes of a mere look something so tangible.

Each time a writer uses an abstract noun a warning voice sounds in his ear. 'That's bound to be pretty vague,' it says. 'Surely there is a more precise way — a concrete way — of saying that.'

Proper Names

'. . . the name of a person, place or . . .'

> Judy in a castle,
> On Castle Hill;
> Cold, November, '67,
> It is
> Almost a love poem
> For you.

Or

> I no longer look like my
> Passport Photograph
> — School Uniform and spots,
>   Huddersfield Station, December —

These are extracts — both marvellous — from the work of students. What lives in a name! Huddersfield.

A writer never misses the chance to call a thing by its *proper* name. And yet the untrained writer is for ever overlooking this most available device for being particular, for defining exactly his authority, for casting exactly his spell, for defining exactly his love.

Read this:

THE STATION'S NAME

> Yes, I remember the station's
> Name — because one afternoon
> Of heat the express train drew up there
> Unwontedly. Like some tune,
>
> The steam hissed. Someone cleared his throat.
> No one left and no one came
> On the bare platform. What I saw
> Was the station's name — just the name —
>
> And trees, and some wild herb, and grass,
> And wild flowers, and haycocks dry;
> No whit less still and lonely fair
> Than the clouds up in the sky.

And for that minute a bird sang
Close by, and round him, mistier
Farther and farther, all the birds
Of the parish and the surrounding shire.

Do you care for it? Do you recognize it? Now read what the poet
actually wrote, and see how the poem comes into focus.

ADLESTROP

Yes, I remember Adlestrop —
The name — because one afternoon
Of heat the express train drew up there
Unwontedly. It was late June.

The steam hissed. Someone cleared his throat.
No one left and no one came
On the bare platform. What I saw
Was Adlestrop — only the name —

And willows, willow-herb, and grass,
And meadowsweet, and haycocks dry;
No whit less still and lonely fair
Than the high cloudlets in the sky.

And for that minute a blackbird sang
Close by, and round him, mistier,
Farther and farther, all the birds
Of Oxfordshire and Gloucestershire.
                                        Edward Thomas

Verbs

Imagine you were around at the moment the rudiments of language
were being discovered. First came the grunts in the shape of names
— MAN. WOMAN. FIRE. Then from outside, MAMMOTH! One
big name, speaking danger. But with it a new need, the need to
name something entirely different. 'What's that mammoth up to?'
The verb was born.

First, no doubt, you simply made a verb out of a noun. When your
children became over excited, you told them not to mammoth
about. We still do that, make verbs out of nouns. In other words,
responding to need, we give drama, or action, to the noun. We *jet*
across the Atlantic, *bomb* Slough and forget to *garage* the car.

Verbs then are names too — '. . . used to express action or being'.
Dependent on nouns, but powerful.

Not so powerful when the mammoth is merely *being*, when for

29

instance he's sleeping (intransitive verb); but when he's *acting*, when for instance he tosses (transitive verb) you over his head, very powerful indeed.

Nouns may be the most loaded words, but verbs are the most dramatic.

Unlike a noun, a verb is a word of parts. It has tenses, and infinitives and participles and gerunds (all of which presumably mean something to the grammarian); and, like a king in a democracy, a verb must agree with its subject. But the question that really concerns the writer is this: do these different parts carry different potencies?

Let's see.

'The mammoth is asleep under the tree.' That expresses a state of being; a calm observation — you might say it gives a false sense of security.

'The mammoth sleeps under the tree.' That's more powerful. You get the feeling that the mammoth is putting his back into it. His sleeping has almost become an act. The reader is put on the alert.

'The mammoth has gone to sleep under the tree.' More powerful still. That really does suggest action. It also points out that the mammoth was awake beforehand. Now the drama's creeping in. He might wake up.

All three statements are in the present. They all say the same thing — to the untuned ear. And that's the point. The tuned ear detects the difference. A difference of meaning, and a difference of power.

The writer then measures not by the rule book but by his ear. The writer must have an ear; and by discipline he must tune it to register where the power, and so the meaning, lies. For instance, he must have trained himself to choose, in every context, the strongest form of the verb that will serve his meaning. It is thus that he writes dramatically, and, as we shall see, every sentence, if it is to be interesting, must be an unfolding drama.

Here are two other examples. They can be used to sharpen the ear.
1. When a writer comes on the ending *-ing* (as in runn*ing*, laugh*ing*, etc.) he reacts with a suspicion similar to that he reserves for abstract nouns: -ing always expresses a state (i.e. the *state* of running) and not an act. So it's less dramatic, and less powerful.

Running down the road he threw a stone at a passing fox.
A fox passed him as he ran down the road. He threw a stone at it.

Obviously a word would not have come into existence if there had been no need for it. But equally, if there were only one way of saying a thing there would be only one writer. We are discussing the

30

situation where there are options.

> He lies at my feet, and is bleeding.
> He lies at my feet, and bleeds.

Do they say the same thing? If not, which is the one you mean? But in any event does your ear catch how the second is more active and immediate, and so in a sense more vital?

2. A verb not only has parts, it has moods. At least that's what the grammarian tells us. The active, the passive and the subjunctive. There's not much discussion to be had about the last, it's use is too specific. But the former two are sometimes interchangeable. Options again; power options. In the active mood the subject is the doer; in the passive he merely gets done. No need to ask which is the more powerful.

So whenever a passive presents itself, the writer is on his guard. 'Steady on, can I make this stronger? Can I turn it round without altering the sense?'

> He fought them to the last, but finally was run through by their spears.
> He fought them to the last. But finally with their spears they ran him through.

In that second one you can practically hear the spears skewering through the flesh.

The Clock

The verb is also the writer's clock. It sets his action in time — in the past, in the present, in the future. Obvious, but it is also subtle. Try describing, say, a visit to the dentist three ways. First from the waiting-room — the tense (tense is the right word) will be the future. Then from the chair — very much the painful present. And last from the street just after you've walked out — all in the past!

Three quite different dramas. Which do you want? Your choice is a choice of tense.

Worrying

The aim of this book is not to list rules, but merely pointers; pointers that will enable the reader to *worry* his or her own work. Yes, just as a dog worries a bone, chewing on it until he gets his tongue on the marrow!

Here is an example of what is meant by 'worrying'. The passage comes from a student's poem about a city girl sitting on a wild, isolated cliff.

> Yet as I lay there
> A feeling of tranquillity
> Unnoticed at first, but
> Slowly gaining in strength
> Was infused into my being by
> The strange lullaby of waves attacking
> The merciless rocks.

The sense is there, but it's like the silver coin at the bottom of the fast brook — one can see the flash come and go but one can't easily put one's finger on it. So now, with the few pointers we've already discussed, we'll *worry* it. Read it again, slowly.

1. 'As I *lay* there . . .' So far, fine: very clear, very strong. A good active use of an inactive transitive verb.
2. 'A feeling . . .' Look out, remember Hopkins, how he said what he felt by describing the wave and not the feeling.
3. 'Tranquillity . . .' The red light's flashing, abstract noun — a real whopper.
4. 'Gain*ing* . . .' Is that all right? Maybe. If you can't use *gained.*
5. 'Strength . . .' For an abstract noun that is quite strong. But is it the right word? *Can* a feeling of tranquillity gain in *strength*? Intensity yes. But strength?
6. 'Was infused . . .' Red light! Passive.
7. 'My being . . .' Of all abstracts that's the craziest! 'A feeling of tranquillity, gaining in strength, was infused into my being . . .' Could she merely mean, 'I felt increasingly tranquil . . .'?
8. 'Lullaby . . .' Ah, now she's talking. One's ear can hear what she says. Lullaby, a song that gives 'a feeling of tranquillity, increasing in strength.'.
9. 'waves . . .' Now she's talking.
10. 'attack*ing* . . .' It may be all right, but watch it.
11. 'rocks.' You can't get much more concrete than that.

Now, with respect, we can tell the author what she might have written:

> I lay there.
> Slowly my ear came alive
> To the thunder
> Three hundred feet below me —

The waves' continuous attack
On the merciless rocks.
A strange lullaby.

That is clear. We could work it further, and will do when we've discussed the Adjective. But at least the meaning is clear. Of course nothing's this easy; there is, as we shall see later, more than meaning that makes for magic in a piece of writing, whether verse or prose. There is also the sound and rhythm of the words. These too we have altered. So the writer can justifiably say, 'Yes, but you have shattered my music.' Here is just one reason why writing is so maddeningly difficult: the clarity of the music *must* be matched by the clarity of the meaning.

There are few writers who do not at times ache to write freed from the wrestle with meaning, and to use words just for their music. But words do mean, and there is no escape. So we must first be able to handle a clear meaning. Then we can start to slap on the colour, the sound and the fury.

Even just the few pointers we've already discussed, the concrete strength of the noun, the active strength of the verb, should enable anyone to produce a piece of work the meaning of which is clearer than the original draft of the above *published* poem.

Suggestions for Practice

1. Compose pairs of sentences to illustrate: a. the weakness of the abstract noun/the strength of the concrete; b. the precision and the power of the proper noun; c. the weakness of the passive/ strength of the active verb; d. the weakness of the -ing ending.
2. Choose a paragraph from some previous composition of your own. Use the pointers from these first four chapters to 'worry' it. Then rewrite it.

Chapter Five

COMPONENTS OF POWER (II)
— Qualifiers

Adjectives

Meanwhile, back in the cave, you have tamed the mammoth. Now you've started to keep cows. They are brown cows, but since in your experience all cows are brown, 'cow' to you means 'brown cow'. Then one day an extraordinary thing happens. A cow gives birth to a *black* calf. You rush back to the cave to tell the folks. But you're stumped — at a loss for a word. There and then you make the move destined to be the bane of all inexperienced writers: you invent the adjective!

There are the two time-honoured definitions of an adjective. First, that it *describes* a noun. Second, that it *qualifies* a noun. It does both.

It's when we consider the adjective that we confront the central insoluble dilemma that makes the writer's job so exacting.

On the one hand he is intent on letting loose with his spells the most power possible; on the other he is intent on being precise and accurate. Often these aims conflict. Here's an example.

In the first chapter we imagined a game of word-response. Suppose that the word chosen had been 'SPIDER', but that instead of calling 'SPIDER', the teacher had been more precise, had said, 'LITTLE RED MONEY SPIDER'. We can say confidently that the range of the response would have been limited. Less power would have been released. Because, by making the noun particular, in other words by qualifying or defining it, only that particular part of the noun's potential would have been tapped.

The one word *spider*, the bare name, rings with full power in the listener's or reader's imagination, and so activates that imagination to respond to the full charge. But qualify the word to *little red money spider* and the shutters come down on the imagination; the imagination then responds only to the qualified meaning.

'Tiger, tiger burning bright . . .' But
'Old, flabby, one-eyed tiger burning bright . . .' . . . You take the point.

So it's true; every adjective *does* qualify its noun. It qualifies the meaning — and it qualifies the power. So avoid them like the poisonous toadstools!

'Hey!'
'I beg your pardon?'
'Poisonous. You just used poisonous. Adjective.'
'Yes, but some toadstools are delicious. Silly to avoid them all.'
'No, you're wrong. Toadstools are poisonous. If you want to eat them you have to eat edible toadstools. You need an adjective to make them edible.'

So the adjective can not only qualify, it can also describe, or make precise. And it's clear that precision also has its power. The naked, unqualified power *or* the power of precision. The writer is constantly spiking his brains on the horns of this dilemma!

There's nothing that sooner reveals a writer's skill, or lack of it, than his use of the adjective. The bad writer simply cannot hear when the adjective is contributing to, as opposed to compromising or merely duplicating, the meaning of a noun. He writes of 'lovely roses' and 'useful utensils', and of 'millepedes with countless legs'. With adjectives he either states the obvious, or else puts truth out of focus.

> If we make a habit of saying 'The true facts are these', we shall come under suspicion when we profess to tell merely 'the facts'.
>
> Sir Ernest Gower

But used by a fine writer the adjective is a word of unrivalled delight. It is adornment, the jewellery, the leaves on the tree. It brings the picture into exact focus; or in other words it focuses the reader's eye exactly as the writer wishes. Read this poem by a student:

BULLS IN A MIST

The bulls stood up as I passed;
Their terrible geopraphies rising from presumed fields.
Each bulk slopped
From tent-pole hips to hang, stuffed laundry-bags,
Between the knees. They turned
And followed me, idle as thugs,

Under the obscene vocabulary of their fringes
Their frontal bones
Could demolish tenements, no, could demolish
Any block post or bastion you could imagine.
The target wrinkles of their eyes
Calculated landslides of concrete. Moreover,
They needed handkerchiefs and bibs,
They needed trousers, but they advanced
Splashing dung, their hairy meteors slack.

Accomplices, they were, of the omniverous mist
That breathed rank recipes and licked my face;
Gate-crashers who'd knock my picnic
Into a cocked hat; ambassadors who'd mash
My silo of ripe intentions into a trough, I knew my place.

Jane Wilson

Look at the adjectives: *presumed* fields, *tent-pole* hips, (note the concrete use of a *noun* as an adjective), *idle* as thugs (note the marvellous way the *noun* is made to describe the adjective!), *omniverous* mist (an adjective with a brilliant double twist), and perhaps best of all — my silo of *ripe* intentions (here the double meaning of the adjective is ironic, and in one flash sums up the self-deriding theme of the whole haunting poem).

That writer, by the power of her *individual* vision (could one doubt for a second that she experienced this), succeeds in conjuring a scene so convincing and so much her own that somehow one feels it to be instantly familiar. That's a paradox. And it is the accomplishment of precisely this paradox, i.e. the use of individual vision to reveal a universal 'familiarity' or truth, the eternity in the grain of sand, that is the aim of all art. She has used adjectives so that they contribute enormously to this success.

It emerges that although ninety-five out of every hundred adjectives on the page warrant the pursuit of criminal proceedings, adjectives can (and that means must) be used to superb effect.

The Adjectival

All that we have said about the adjective can be applied in exactly the same way to adjectival phrases or clauses or pieces of the verb.

The sun, *now my alarm clock,* rose at six.
The bomb, *which had ticked erratically all night,* finally blew up at day-break.
The *plummeting* barometer presaged a storm.

Whenever any one of them occurs that same red light is flashing on the dashboard. It may be no more than a caution, but get used to seeing it and heeding it. Is the noun's power being compromised unnecessarily? What in context would be lost without these qualifications — would the sentence be more powerful, more dramatic?

The sun rose at six.
The bomb blew up at dawn.
The barometer presaged storm.

One can't argue but that these statements are more concise, more powerful. But, and here's the old dilemma again, in each case something indispensable has been lost. Maybe there's no solution. But maybe there is. Maybe there are hundreds. In any event, notice how in each case if we make *two* sentences, which essentially means involving a second main verb, we can preserve the sense exactly, but intensify the drama:

The sun rose at six. It was my alarm clock.
All night the bomb ticked erratically. At daybreak it blew up.
The barometer plummeted. It presaged a storm.

Just a moment! With that last one, we may have stumbled on the final solution. All that guff about the storm — we don't need it, it's like a bad adjective. It's an insult to the reader. So we're left with:

The barometer plummeted.

Now we're writing!

Adverbs

Graham Green has expressed the opinion that the adverb is even more dangerous than the adjective. That's a caution to be heeded. The adverb is to the verb as the adjective is to the noun. It exists, of course, because there's an important role for it; but it is dangerous. It has the same tendency, i.e. that in describing it qualifies, and that in qualifying it weakens.

'The mouse scampered *hurriedly* back to its hole.' By now your ear should be telling you how that adverb insults the verb; it insists on tagging along but in fact it has nothing to add to the strength or meaning of the verb, and it doesn't make it more particular. So it's a parasite; it weakens it. It's like the fairy-tale goblin who offers to help the woodcutter carry the tree-trunk up the hill, but behind the man's back merely leaps astride and takes a free ride.

37

But they can be used well. Remember D.H. Lawrence's snake?

> He drank enough
> And lifted his head, *dreamily*, as one who has drunken,

With that one word, set so tellingly apart, the entire image shifts, from the factual, into slow-time and reverie. Beautifully done.

The adverb, needless to say, has its *adverbial*: a tricky region where if you're not careful you're in the power of the dreaded grammarian. Consecutive clauses, concessive clauses, and so forth. But those same dangers exist.

And the same possibilities. Look how Robert Frost describes the way to climb a birch tree.

> He always kept his poise
> To the top branches, climbing carefully
> With the same pains you use to fill a cup
> Up to the brim, and even above the brim.

Or the astonishingly subtle way this student twists his 'cinema' image into further life by extending *adverbially* the sense of *reels*:

> Almost a black poem
> For your hand in the cinema —
> Life reels away
> Till the screen is blank —
> And the hand grasps
> Only air.

Prepositions

There's something likeable about prepositions — stocky, independent little words. Full of purpose and self-assurance. No deceit, no hidden dangers, no nonsense. Good friends to the writer.

Most often they form a lever between a verb and a noun — they'd need to be strong for that! 'The stone flew *through* the window.' They give a particular focus to a verb; they qualify, but they don't weaken.

> The gull flew *out from* and *down* the cliff.

You see how they can be used to give two distinct motions to a single verb? In fact they are so volatile that they can even dispense with the verb altogether.

> Right lads, *into* the house!
> Out brief candle!

Pronouns, Conjunctions and Interjections

Pronouns: clearly there have to be pronouns; without them how would *I* ever communicate with *you?*

Conjunctions: little words, and yet invaluable. *But* was Dr Johnson's favourite word.

Interjections: Crumbs and *Good grief!* Without them the Beano and Charlie Brown would be out of business.

And that's the lot.

Something Else to Worry About . . .

Alive in particular to the dangers of adjectives and adverbs, we'll worry our way through another student's poem:

NO-MAN'S LAND

A forgotten swing rocks
silently and mechanically.
Discarded bales of rotting hay
lies as ruins
along with the battered sign saying —
'Scotland Farm. No Trespass.'

There's a rust mangled tractor
surrounded by ragged barbed wires.
Where's that milk bottle crawling on its side
and the gnarled paper come from?
Solitary farm,
detached, fulfilled and existing: no-man's land.
Solitary farm, which wants no visitors.

However practised or unpractised this writer is with the written word, there's clearly nothing wrong with her sensitivity to places. Perhaps though, if she'd just read these last two chapters, she'd have viewed this as an early draft, and been able then to submit it to something like the following treatment:

1. *forgotten,* caution! Adjective. Forgotten by whom? Does she *know* it's forgotten? Could be all right; we'll see.
2. *rocks* . . . That's not right, *rocks* implies 'resting on a fulcrum'. A swing implies suspension. A swing *swings!* But she can't say that — which is why she had to make do with *rocks.* What a dilemma!

3. *silently and mechanically.* Look out, adverbs! And anyway there's something odd here, a confusion. Firstly, silence and mechanism seem, though are not necessarily, at odds. The only mechanism ever to drive a swing is a boy or a girl. Surely this was the wind? The wind, whatever else, is not mechanical. Better have another look at the swing.
4. *Discarded . . . rotting . . . as ruins . . .* all qualifiers all describing much the same thing. Almost certainly there'll be a more concise and powerful way of expressing this.

> Good writers are those who keep the language efficient. That is to say, keep it accurate, keep it clear.
>
> Ezra Pound

5. *along with.* Does it really help to extend that image to the *battered sign* . . . does it not just confuse, or put out of focus?
6. *Saying . . .* Come off it, a sign doesn't say; if anything it *sign*ifies!
7. *rust mangled . . .* No! rust does *not* mangle.
8. *surrounded by . . .* 'We would ask you to tell us something more interesting about the relationship between the tractor and the wire.'

> How forcible are right words
>
> Old Testament

9. *ragged barbed wires.* That *ragged* is criminal: it actually *blunts* the barbed wire.
10. *Where's that . . .* the following two lines, with their faulty grammar, are nearly strong: but again just out of focus. This *crawling on its side,* is it actually moving? Or is it crawling with insects or something? Maybe to describe them will be enough; the reader will do his own wondering where they come from.
11. *Solitary . . .* Adjective! Yes, but it's beautiful. Its double meaning and its own 'solitari*ness*' give it a marvellous tang.
12. *detached, fulfilled and existing . . .* First, be good enough to tell us what *detached* adds to *solitary.* And then, quite simply, what, on earth, is meant by *fulfilled and existing.* In fact we already *know* what's meant because we've read the rest of the poem — so

don't say anything so fatuous.
13. *no-man's land* . . . two-edged and good.
14. *Solitary farm* . . . Do we really need it again? It was so good
    once, but does repeating it add anything? More likely it just
    becomes blunt with use.
15. *which wants no visitors.* Here's a real dilemma. Just what does
    she mean? If she means by *wants, lacks* (i.e. lacks no visitors),
    then that's fine. Very good in fact. It suggests ghosts, and strange
    presences like Walter de la Mare's Listeners. But how's the
    reader to know it doesn't mean *desires* no visitors? That would be
    bad, that would be committing what's called 'pathetic fallacy', in
    other words belittling this solitary farm by attributing to it the
    feelings of a mere human-being! Can one risk it? After all it adds
    very little to what's been said.
If the author had done that, what might she have come up with?

NO-MAN'S LAND

The swing
silently swinging.
Bales of hay in ruins.
A battered notice:
Scotland Farm. No Trespassers.
The tractor rusted
mangled
penned by barbed wire,
a milk bottle, crawling,
and gnarled paper.
Solitary farm —
vital no-man's land.

And even that *vital.* Does it add anything, or just detract?
We've worried it from 64 words to 36. Does it say what the writer
wanted to say? We can't know. Does it say as much as the original?
Probably not, and yet often it is by saying less that we are able to say
more. One thing is certain — it is more precise, and therefore, in
one sense, it is better written.

Suggestions for Practice

1. There follow two extracts from student's work. Consider whether,
   and if so how, they may be worried to a more concise, more
   powerful form.

   (i) Your eyes, piercing penetrating pools,
       Swimming, swirling into my mind,

My whole being, infinitely fathomless.
My mind lies naked to your gaze,

Yours is locked and encased, closed to everyone,
Everyone, even you.

(ii)   The old woman reached out a trembling frail hand and
lovingly caressed a faded well-worn photo, and two full
tears slid slowly away from their source.

2. Write two descriptions of say *a face* or a *sunset* (not more than a
hundred words to each), the first using any means available, but
the second without adjectives or abstract nouns or adverbs.
3. Choose three adjectives or adverbs and compose for each a pair
of sentences which illustrate how they can (i) strengthen and
(ii) weaken the words they qualify.
4. Take at random one of your old compositions. Make a count of
the adjectives and adverbs. Then count the number that either
weaken or else do not alter the meaning.

Chapter Six

THE IMAGE

The image, is a device — in fact of all those available to the writer it is the most powerful. No surprise then, after what has been said in the previous chapter, that the image is a device for expressing something in language that is comprehensible to one or more of the five senses. It is by means of the senses that we register what is conveyed by the image.

Strictly, of course, image refers to something visual. But we're giving it a slightly wider meaning: one or more words which conjure(s) an immediate impression to sight, or hearing, or scent, or touch, or taste; or, as with the 'finger-lickin' good' that describes a certain fried chicken, some combination of the five.

The writer can employ imagery to deliver or express different levels of meaning. To explore this let's, for a minute, go back to the sorcerer or magician.

Traditionally one of the elementary sources of the magician's power is his knowledge that each object has to its one name three quite separate identities (or, if you like, three quite separate names):

First, it is an *individual*: Say an individual cat, quite unlike any other cat.

Second, it is a representative of its genus, or type of family, i.e. it is a member of that particular branch of mammals called *cats* (tiger, tabby). On this level its attributes aren't individual, but common to all cats.

Thirdly, it has its magical, or original, or universal, identity. On this level the name carries the power of symbol, it embodies the original and constant essence of each and every cat; it symbolizes all, and that means more than we can otherwise express, that is *catty* — the secret of what is *cat-like*.

Now, what happens when we use these three identities as a measure of the writer's various use of imagery?

Examples:
1. And Pepper, her own, her very own cat, had climbed up his coat, and now lay on his shoulder, purring feebly.

2. He was typically a Persian cat, blue-haired and yellow-eyed, a creature of smoke and fire, of grey jade and topaz, who sits upon a wall and receives tribute daily, looking past his worshippers' heads with subtle shining eyes like those of an idol staring over priests in an Eastern temple.

Morley Roberts from *The Young Man Who Stroked Cats*

3. In the silence of the watching we heard something without mewing like a she-otter. We both rose to our feet, and, I answer for myself, not Strickland, felt sick — actually and physically sick. We told each other, as did the men in Pinafore, that it was the cat.

Rudyard Kipling from *The Mark of the Beast*

We could argue about the relative power of the first two. But about the third, no argument. Here the explosion of meaning is so powerful it cannot be fully contained by the conscious mind, but carries down deep and moves us somewhere else. In other words in that area which responds to the full charge of language, to spell and symbol, namely the imagination.

> The Fable of the Poet and the Blonde Symbol. The Poet invited this Symbol out to supper, because she had long blonde hair, long legs and a long history. She lived in a small but elegant apartment in Knightsbridge, and, at seven one evening, the Poet rang her bell. The door opened and out stepped the Symbol clad in nothing but her natural mystery. "Good God," said the Poet, "I can't take you out like that. Why, you've got no words on at all. You will be arrested for indecent exposure." So they retired upstairs and studied the meaning of meaning.
>
> George Barker

These three examples are in prose. The image, though, is a device effective in every form of writing from advertisement to epic. But maybe we should expect that a poet's concern will require that his imagery is the most exact, the most intense, and like laser-beams the most burningly focused. Let's then see what's to be learned by compiling a short inventory of types of image as used by poets.

The Direct Descriptive Image

Shakespeare's famous and incredible:

> The barge she sat in, like a burnished throne,
> Burnt on the water; the poop was beaten gold;
> Purple the sails; and so perfumed that
> The winds were love-sick with them . . . .

Any scholar worth his salt could, no doubt, produce a volume of reasons why that is more than merely a description. But as far as writers are concerned it *is* merely descriptive. The great writer looks at the thing as it was or may have been, does it over with his eye, and makes gold of it so that for his audience it is cast in the currency of the imagination. In other words he upgrades it from identity 1 to 3, from a common particular to a particular universal.

Or Tennyson's:

> Miriads of rivulets hurrying through the lawn,
> The moan of doves in immemorial elms,
> And murmur of innumerable bees.

A *sound* image if ever there was one (and we'll have more discussion about sound in chapter 8), but merely descriptive.

The Narrative Image

Roger Garfitt's:

> The clocked-in hours have ticked to a close
> and we've streamed out, dunking our cards
> in the machine, to the works buses,
> lit up *the longest cigarette of the day.*

More or less straight description until we get to that cigarette. It is narrative because it catches that moment of the day when one breathes deep and enjoys the cigarette to the full. The whole day unfolds, past, present and future.

And this by George Mackey Brown:

HORSE

> The horse at the shore
> Casks of red apples, skull, a barrel of rum.

> The horse in the field
> Plough, ploughman, gulls, a furrow, a cornstalk.

> The horse in the peat-bog
> Twelve baskets of dark fire

The horse at the pier
Letters, bread, paraffin, one passenger, papers

The horse at the show
Ribbons, raffia, high bright hooves

The horse in the meadow
A stallion, a red wind, between the hills

A horse at the burn
Quenching a long flame in the throat

Writing does not come more concrete. Yet feel how each description runs beyond itself so that it becomes narrative not just of moments, but of days and whole lives.

The Transforming Image

Read this deceptively simple poem by A. E. Housman:

LOVELIEST OF TREES

Loveliest of trees, the cherry now
Is hung with bloom along the bough,
And stands about the woodland ride
Wearing white for Eastertide.

Now, of my three-score years and ten,
Twenty will not come again,
And take from seventy springs a score,
It only leaves me fifty more.

And since to look at things in bloom
Fifty springs are little room,
About the woodlands I will go
To see the cherry hung with snow.

We're in fact called to look at a single image, a flowering cherry. At first out of focus, *bloom*, he conceals whether it is pink or white. Then it explodes *white* with all the triumphant attributes of Easter. In the centre the image gives way to a riddle: how old is he? But then returns, leading to the final note, which *is* the poem, *snow*. We are dazzled by the flash of white, and maybe leave it at that, and so fail to consider why it is that finally we have been moved by strange heart-ache. *Snow,* all in that word the cold visitant; snow, the white flowering of winter, lingering a day or two until it melts away in the first sunlight, in summer no more than a cutting memory. In one exact conjuring the cherry-bloom has in our imaginations been set in living relief; it has received the *identity* of snow. It is that magic that moves us.

Plato said that the distinguishing gift of the poet is his ability to see similarities in dissimilar objects. In other words, the power of *metaphor*. He had good reason. Nowhere else is the magic so clearly revealed. The poet with his sharpened senses *sees* in things their secret. Calling one by name he summons its secret and then imprints it on the secret identity of another. Now deep down, down where things discover their origins, the latter suffers this elemental transmutation; in other words the thing *is* changed, and its identity is renewed and enriched.

> Above all things else, we must recall, *the imagination is an assimilating energy.* It pierces through dissimilarity to some underlying oneness in which qualities the most remote cohere . . .
>
> G. L. Lowes

The spell is cast. The prince is changed into the frog. It'll take a woman's kiss to restore him — but that's another magic.
Brian Patten:

> Then perhaps it is best that we wake expecting little,
> feel no more need to exaggerate ourselves
> nor perform those rituals that have ceased to amaze us,
> but washed by the morning's first light
> to drift out into the city, one thought
> in its still sleeping brain . . .

That is beautiful, and telling — about us and the city, about thoughts and the brain. We see that for such an image to succeed it must have two properties. First it must be *shocking*; it must make the reader catch his breath in surprise. Second, it must be *appropriate*, the likeness must be true and telling. If it's untrue the writer is as bad at his job and as misleading as an electrician who gets the wires mixed in a plug.

Here's another transformer, W. H. Davies:

> . . . I turned my head and saw the wind,
>   No far from where I stood,
>   Dragging the corn by her golden hair,
>   Into a dark and lonely wood.

Only someone alien to the countryside could find that image sentimental and far-fetched. There's nothing more tender and feminine than a field of ripe corn. The wind across the field *does* appear as a cold shadow dragging the corn. There's nothing so dank, sullen and watchful as the silence in a summer wood on a windy day. Exact magic.

The Magic Image

In fact this isn't a category. But it allows us to include a student's remarkable poem that makes its own point. Namely, that if only we will *see,* the whole stable world becomes fluid, susceptible to our magic, to the raids of our imagination.

IMAGES (Cyprus 1961)

The world is troubled
With a lack of looking.
I sing my songs.
The world sleeps.

I see the sky reflected in my teacup.
I move the cup
and I tilt the sky.

The flying crane is shadowed
On the mud wall.
My shadow touches his
And I ride the bird.

The stars are mirrored in a pool
Of rain.
With my hand I scoop up the water.
I have a handful of stars.

I grasp the branch of a tree.
The wind blows
And the tree shakes my hand.

The moon shimmers on my glass of cognac.
I drink
And taste the moon.

I climb a fig tree and look down.
The earth has fallen.

My mother's face appears
On the surface of an olive.
I split the olive
And scar my mother's face.

All the world
All the world pours in at my barred window.
I lower my lids
And dam the flood.

George Tardios

The Fiery Image

This is the image we feel to have no earthly source, but seems to have sprung on the mind of the visionary poet direct from the intense world of the imagination. One hesitates before mentioning the phenomenon in a manual dedicated to the practical and measurable. However not to mention it is to turn one's back on the mystery which underlies everything that is challenging and enlivening about the art of writing.

> Tyger, tyger, burning bright
> In the forests of the night
> What immortal hand or eye
> Dare frame thy fearful symmetry?

The forests of the night . . . how could the mind cope! And yet it speaks to us; it disturbs us, somewhere. Even it seems to speak of a world we dimly remember . . . But note that not even here, or perhaps here least of all, is there anything abstract.

The writer when he commands this imagery, whether it is in verse or prose, assumes arguably the highest office; and then his eye, as Shakespeare describes it,

> . . . in a fine frenzy rolling,
> Doth glance from heaven to earth, from earth to heaven;
> And as imagination bodies forth
> The forms of things unknown, the poet's pen
> Turns them to shapes, and gives to airy nothing
> A local habitation and a name.

It is in this 'fine frenzy' that he becomes, as William Blake knew probably as well as any since Merlin left for the woods, the author of revelation and prophecy:

> Hear the voice of the Bard!
> Who Present, Past and Future sees
> Whose ears have heard,
> The Holy Word,
> That walked among the ancient trees.

We are all different at the moment when imagination takes us and sets aside our devious daily minds so that we come up with an image that goes right to the exact core of what we have to say. We surpass the mundane in ourselves. The great writer has learned how he can put himself and his skills in the possession of the imagination; but in random moments of so-called gold the imagination may claim any of us, and at that moment we utter as Thomas the Rhymer back from Elfland, with 'the tongue that can never lie'.

The Arresting Image

This is the image devised by a good writer to make acceptable to the *senses* a theme which would be otherwise too abstract. Andrew Marvell in his majestic poem 'The Definition of Love', finds himself bound to tangle with just about every abstraction in the book. But look how he copes with it:

> Magnanimous Despair alone
> Could show me so divine a thing,
> Where feeble Hope could ne'r have flown
> But vainly flapt its Tinsel Wing.

Interesting how for Marvell and poets of that time all nouns are *names* to be honoured with a capital letter.

Another example of how to make the abstract tangible is Thomas Wyatt's superb poem of despair. It needs no comments:

> My galy charged with forgetfulness
> Thorrough sharpe sees in wynter nyghtes doeth pas
> Twene Rock and Rock; and eke myn ennemy, Alas,
> That is my lorde, sterith with cruelnes;
> And every owre (oar) a thought in redines,
> As tho that deth were light in suche a case.
> An endles wynd doeth tere the sayll apase
> Of forced sightes and trusty ferefulnes.
> A rain of teris (tears), a clowde of dark disdain,
> Hath done the wered cordes great hinderaunce;
> Wrethed with errour and eke with ignoraunce.
> The starres be hid that led me to this pain;
> Drowned is reason that should me consort,
> And I remain dispering of the port.

If any one, at this point, is tempted to think the arresting image the exclusive property of the lyric poet, let him consider these:

The first is from a play. The playwright uses image in exactly the same way to make the abstract passion tangible and specific, but also to expand his drama, to take it as it were beyond his character:

As I write this a swallow
weaves towards my window,
　I notice its restless grace:
A month ago, I would not even have seen it.
My eyes were blind to anything that was not you.
But now, on the wings of this bird
　The whole of creation flies to me!
For the first time, I am alive
　Now that I am dead to myself:
I can be to you,
　I can be to them,
　　I can even be to things.
　　　Ronald Duncan from *Heloise to Abelard*

The second from a novel. And to what effect we'll leave you to judge:

Then they went into Jose Arcadio Buendia's room, shook him as hard as they could, shouted in his ear, put a mirror in front of his nostrils, but they could not awaken him. A short time later, when the carpenter was taking measurements for the coffin, through the window they saw a light rain of tiny yellow flowers falling. They fell on the town all through the night in a silent storm, and they covered the roofs and blocked the doors and smothered the animals who slept outdoors. So many flowers fell from the sky that in the morning the streets were carpeted with a compact cushion and they had to clear them away with shovels and rakes so that the funeral procession could pass by.
　　Gabriel Garcia Marquez *One Hundred Years of Solitude*

Three Figures of Speech

You could argue — and Carlyle did — that all language, since it makes meaning available to the ear, is a form of metaphor. But at the same time a metaphor is among a number of clearly defined figures of speech, or forms of image. To sum up the chapter we'll look at three of these, and measure their potential for the writer.

Of all, the *metaphor* is the most powerful. Here the writer doesn't liken one thing to another. He simply takes the identity of one thing and *imprints* it on another — and so perpetrates magic.

In Robert Frost's 'Bereft' it's a windy day and

Out on the porch's sagging floor,
Leaves got up in a coil and hissed,
Blindly struck at my knee and missed.

Without mentioning the snake, the snake is there *and* all that day's malevolence.

In our own English compositions he showed no mercy to phrase, metaphor, or image, unsupported by a sound sense, or where the same sense might have been conveyed with equal force and dignity in plainer words. Lute, Harp, and Lyre, Muse, Muses and Inspirations, Pegasus, Parnassus, and Hippocrene were all an abomination to him. In fancy I can almost hear him now, exclaiming, "Harp? Harp? Lyre? Pen and ink, boy, you mean! Muse, boy, Muse? Your nurse's daughter, you mean! Pierian spring? Oh aye! the cloister-pump, I suppose!"

S. T. Coleridge

The *simile* does liken. And for this very reason it seems somehow to be weaker. One is made aware of the device, and so it becomes self-conscious. Its danger is that it tends to be 'arty' or artificial. Just how *good* is

O my luve is like a red, red rose,
That's newly sprung in June . . . ?

Well, of course it's wonderful — because Burns is a great magician. But in fact it would need to be magic, because without the magic it is a pretty fatuous statement.

But simile, finely used, *can* take on the inevitability and purpose of metaphor:

THE DARK HILLS

Dark hills at evening in the west,
Where sunset hovers like a sound
Of golden horns that sang to rest
Old bones of warriors under ground,
Far now from all the bannered ways
Where flash the legions of the sun,
You fade — as if the last of days
Were fading, and all wars were done.

Edwin Arlington Robinson

The first simile — a scientist might admire the magic that can work on the vibration of colour and produce sound.

It may be that nowadays simile finds its most effective place in prose-fiction, as if the more vernacular setting is better able to dispel any air of conscious contrivance. But here too, if it is to serve a genuine function and not be mere lornment for its own sake, it requires the very surest touch. As with this, from the hand of Carson McCullers,

> Very slowly he closed his eyelids, and the gesture was like a curtain drawn at the end of a scene in a play.
>
> from *A Tree, A Rock, A Cloud*

To have achieved that same effect by explanation would have entailed goodness knows how many lines of prose. And that concision which bypasses the mind and goes loaded straight to the heart would have been lost.

With *personification* again the writer can make the abstract appear tangible and familiar. And maybe the secret lies in what Blake tells us; that

> Cruelty has a Human Heart
> And Jealousy a Human Face . . . etc.

But today the personification seems out of fashion. We tend to find it too high-flown, and perhaps that it reeks a little of the 'pathetic fallacy'. Still, as we saw, Marvell could make wonderful use of it. Now try this one from Alexander Pope:

> Black Melancholy sits, and round her throws
> A death-like silence and a dead repose;
> Her gloomy prese ice saddens all the scene,
> Shades every flow :r and darkens every green,
> Deepens the murmur of the falling floods
> And breathes a browner horror on the woods.

What about that last line for a 'tactile' metaphor!

The Irish Bull

Shun, of course, the *mixed* metaphor:

> Miss Blank also goes in for portraiture. In hitting off her Father's head her intentions are good, but the execution lacks very much in artistic finish.
>
> *Dorchester Gazette*

Exactly! Get your magic wrong and you may well commit murder. But the Irish Bull is altogether something else.

P. Grierson, who wrote a treatise on this beast, tells us that 'an Irish Bull possesses some ethereal quality denied to bulls of other races! Why should we doubt it? Sir Boyle Roche was its great champion. He once warned the Speaker of the Irish House of Commons, 'Here perhaps, Sir, the murderous Marshal Law men will break in, cut us to mincemeat, and throw our bleeding heads upon the table to stare us in the face.'

Grierson quotes the authority of Mahaffy: 'The chief characteristic of an Irish Bull is that it is always pregnant.' Amen. A fine figure of speech.

Suggestions for Practice

Take at random or invent five startling images. Then write a short piece of prose or verse in which all these five images are included.

Chapter Seven

SYNTAX or a CONNECTED ORDER OF THINGS

Syntax

Look up the word syntax in a good dictionary. There are several meanings. You'll see that at some point the grammar-pundits stole it: 'the department of grammar which deals with the established usages of grammatical construction and the rules deduced therefrom.' Yes, just what one feared. But then there is an older meaning. Simply; 'A connected order or system of things.' That meaning is obsolete, gone from use, which is a pity because to a writer it makes real sense. Come to think of it, that's an even better definition: Good syntax makes real sense.

> I wish our clever young poets would remember my homely definitions of prose and poetry, that is, prose — words in their best order; poetry — the best words in their best order.
>
> S. T. Coleridge

Testimonial in Seedsman's Catalogue: 'I am very pleased with the lot of seeds I got from you recently. Everyone nearly came up.'

Next year he wonders why he's bankrupt. After all the words are fine. It's just that one is in the wrong place.

To many writers, syntax holds a fascination second only to that of the words themselves. Syntax is getting the spell right.

The Dramatic Sentence

Syntax controls two essential aspects of the sentence. First, the meaning; second, the drama.

A sentence dramatic? Yes, and this drama is the key to all effective writing.

Imagine a three-act play, a thriller. In the first act the crime is committed. In the second the private-eye makes his investigation. In the third the criminal is discovered. Now suppose the writer puts the third act second. In that case the audience leaves in the second interval — the drama is over, there is nothing left to hold their interest. The writer has got his 'connected order of things', his syntax, wrong.

Look at a sentence, a simple one: 'The cow jumped over the moon.'

Now see how scene by scene the drama unfolds or, put another way, how word by word the information is conveyed.

The cow
jumped
over
the moon

Suddenly one sees that it *is* a dramatic sentence. The way the meaning unfolds is exciting, both clear and dramatic. The syntax is good.

One might have said, 'Over the moon jumped the cow.' Maybe that's all right too, but here the mind has to stagger after the sense.

But suppose one wants to say a bit more, that this took place on a foggy night. 'The cow jumped over the moon one foggy night.' There the syntax is shoddy. The drama is all finished, when suddenly there's another scene tagged on the end. Not that the audience sees it, they've gone home. Because the phrase is in the wrong place the mind does not register it. The whole balance of the sentence is upset. *But* if one had said, 'One foggy night the cow jumped over the moon' — or even, 'The cow, one foggy night, jumped over the moon.'

Make 'em laugh; make 'em cry; make 'em wait.
Recipe for a bestseller. Charles Reade

We've all experienced the difference between a good and bad story-teller. The two tell the same story, even use the same words. One holds us spellbound. The other — so what! It's all a matter of order, of syntax. The order gives the *emphasis*. The emphasis *is* the drama. The drama *is* the story.

Precisely that difference exists between the good and the bad writer in their treatment of a sentence. They may use the same words. But the good writer has the gift of plot. By his exact ordering of the words he achieves these three things:

1. Clarity of meaning.
2. Logical unfolding of plot.
3. That sense of drama which gives all good writing interest and life.

A writer must have a gift for words. He must also have the gift for good syntax. In a way it is the same gift — it is all in the ear. As with all important gifts, the gift for good syntax does not come gift-wrapped; it must be nurtured and developed — by guidance, and by constant practice. By developing the ear.

Read this:

That, down on the banks of the Gumti, was when, having got over the gate, through a whole day, he pleaded with the lama who set like a flint his face against it, averring that the time had not yet come; pleaded that the next holidays he accompany him on the Road — for a month — for a little week.

And now read what Kipling, who is one of the greatest masters of the narrative sentence, in fact wrote. Read it as we read 'the cow jumped over the moon', watching how the sense unfolds — how the clauses and phrases follow one another with an ease and logic that is spell-binding.

'That was when he got over the gate and pleaded with the lama through the whole day down the banks of the Gumti to accompany him on the Road next holidays — for one month — for a little week; and the lama set his face as a flint against it, averring that the time had not yet come.

Notice how the syntax suggests the pleading; and how the stern character of the lama comes alive. It looks so simple: that is the crowning achievement.

So it is that every sentence we write should constitute a dramatic unfolding. When one does catch it, the finely turned sentence, that is one of the greatest satisfactions of the writer. It is very much like that of a batsman who, his timing perfect, catches the ball on the meat of the bat.

Words carry the power, but it is the syntax that controls the spell.

A Few Dramas

With each of these examples, feel for the plot.

Descartes: 'I think, therefore I am.' Actually he wrote it in Latin

— the language which holds the key to much fine syntax. But imagine if he'd written: 'I am because I think.' What a squelch. All the crescendo is gone. They'd have closed the theatre the first night. Or should that read the first night they'd have closed the theatre?
Ernest Hemingway:

> Living was a horse between your legs and a carbine under one leg and a hill and a valley and a stream with trees along it and the far side of the valley and the hills beyond.

Spectacular. Simply by the syntax (and note there is no punctuation to impede the pace) you're onto that horse and away like the wind over the foreground and into the distance.
Shelley's Ozymandias:

> Round the decay
> Of that colossal wreck, boundless and bare,
> The lone and level sands stretch far away.

He achieves his drama by having the reader's eye, following the syntax, roam away from the broken statue in the foreground and out until the focus becomes vague in the distant immeasurable waste.
John Donne, in his last sermon:

> Even those bodies that were the temple of the Holy Ghost come to this dilapidation, to ruin, to rubbish, to dust.

One short sentence effectively traces the gradual process of total disintegration.
There's a similar achievement in this marvellous sentence by the philosopher J.S. Mill. Note how the sense is heightened by the complementary drama that leads to the final explosion of desolation:

> Thus the mind itself is bowed to the yoke; even in what people do for pleasure conforming is the first thing thought of; they like crowds; they exercise choice only among things commonly done; peculiarity of taste, eccentricity of conduct, are shunned equally with crimes; until by dint of not following their own nature they have no nature to follow; their human capacities are withered and starved.

Or would 'starved and withered' have been better?

To be able to control syntax exactly within a tight verse-form is an achievement equivalent to crossing the Niagara Falls on a tight rope, without a safety-net, and stopping halfway to do up one's bootlace. For these gymnastics our gold medal goes to Alexander Pope. Here's an example. He says he's proud — look how he then proceeds, albeit with the satirist's twist, to steal God's thunder:

Yes, I am proud; I must be proud to see
Men not afraid of God, afraid of me.

Then what about this for dramatic syntax. A Roger McGough special:

A left to the chin
and Winter's down!
1 Tomatoes
2 Radish
3 Cucumber
4 Onions
5 Beetroot
6 Celery
7 and any
8 amount
9 of lettuce
10 for dinner
Winter's out for the count
Spring is the winner!

And the last word from Shakespeare:

Life's but a walking shadow; a poor player,
Who struts and frets his hour upon the stage,
And then is heard no more: it is a tale
Told by an idiot, full of sound and fury,
Signifying nothing . . .

How superbly this syntax, leading through its 'sound and fury' down to the stark abrupt conclusion of nothing, mirrors Macbeth's disillusionment and final total rejection of life.

Solution through Syntax

Here is a student's poem:

A small cotton wool slug
lay, half hidden by the twisted branches,
among the humus,
planted in an instinctive act;
and the eggs lay embedded in their sleep
waiting on torn bark,
created only to achieve life,
plucked by my hand without thought.

Even now as they lay on the table,
the white modern clinical table,
they, already half forgotten, die
while we look on and listen.
What did I know of their purpose?
What right did I have to interfere?
They would have grown
had I not stumbled here.

A more experienced writer might say, 'That's fine, but it's just not in focus. Let's look at the syntax. Get the syntax right, and one often sees at once what's cluttering up the vision.' After worrying a while he might fetch up with this:

Among the humus,
half-hidden by the twisted branches,
lay a small cotton-wool slug.
And waiting on torn bark
lay the eggs
embedded in their sleep.
My hand, without a thought, plucked them.

Now half-forgotten
on the table
the white modern clinical table
while we look on and listen
they die.

In an earlier exercise we took a blurred piece of work, and found for it clarity, and so strength, merely by making the nouns and verbs (the names) strong. Later we did the same by removing any cluttering adjectives and adverbs (qualifiers). Now we've done it simply overhauling the syntax. It seems there is plenty to work with!

> Uncontrolled poetry has no character — and carefully worked-on poetry seems spontaneous and has style.
> Kathleen Raine

What we have achieved here may not be the poem the student was after, but at least now it is clean and emphatic. We have cut it. And now that the syntax is clear we are able to see that what's been cut was just the padding, the attempt to bolster a shoddy statement. Almost always such padding is made up of little bits of unnecessary subjective commentary. For instance, what on earth does 'planted in an instinctive act' contribute? For that matter, what does it mean? The point is that a poem or a story must exist on its own. It must be beyond opinion. By trumping it up with opinions and comments and interpretations, you belabour it. By voicing your opinions you are making the claim that *they* are important and that *you* are important, and that detracts from the writing. It trivializes the work and insults your reader. Just give him the poem or the story and leave him to come up with his own opinions.

Look, now this poem is clean, how beautiful is the line, 'embedded in their sleep'; and how telling and poignant are the poem's last two words. The poem has fallen into place.

Two Monsters of Depravity

Anyone who has read Denys Parsons' collections of misprints and miscastings from newspapers and books will know what amazing worlds any writer, careless just for a moment, may fetch up in.

> At Woodford people were pouring out of trolley buses into Epping Forest, looking green and lovely.
>
> *Evening Standard*

Or

> The Countess of Blank who was with a merry party wore nothing to indicate that she was the holder of four Scottish titles.
>
> Scottish Paper

The collection also illustrates unforgettably the two crimes of syntax most easy to commit. The first is the 'run-on' sentence. This monstrosity is a hybrid like the centaur — its front and its back have no proper connection. It usually happens when a bad writer tries to cram into the one sentence information that is esssentially unrelated. And look what can happen!

> The many friends of Canon T... will be glad to hear that whilst he has somewhat recovered from his long illness, he is still not allowed to take part in any work, and remains confined to his house.
>
> *East Anglian Daily Times*

Or

> The eminent statistician rubbed his ear thoughtfully and produced a cigarette.
>
> From a short story

The other is a beast which at one time in America went by the fearsome title of the 'dangling modifier'. This is a descriptive word, phrase or clause which, by getting out of place and latching onto the wrong subject, can make the most terrible mischief. We see it all too commonly, as in a sentence like, 'I only play golf on Sunday', by which of course is meant, 'I play golf only on Sundays'. Not very terrible. No, but again look what *can* happen.

Our picture shows Mr Robert Tenter rolling the lawn with his fiance, Miss Elizabeth Briarcliffe.

Bucks Paper

or this headline from a Texas Newspaper:

WOMAN HURT WHILE COOKING HER HUSBAND'S BREAKFAST IN A HORRIBLE MANNER

Punctuation

There is an ancient practical teaching that says that there is *nothing* a man *may* not do provided he *knows* (and here that word carries the sense of absolute responsibility) what he is doing. That goes for the art of writing.

Nowhere is this more clearly demonstrated than in the subsiduary art of punctuation.

There are various punctuation marks, and we do well to know them and to be practised in their use . . . after all you cannot safely dispense with something until you have mastered it. But because writing is an *individual* affair, we cannot by learning rules learn to punctuate. For instance what rule is there that commanded Hemingway, in that sentence quoted earlier in the chapter, to omit *all* punctuation?

We have seen that a writer, however perverse, is concerned with a contrivance of power. We've stressed that the more intense the feeling or meaning he is trying to convey, the more important it is that he gets his spell right (look up *spell* in a good dictionary; and while you're about it have a look at *gospel*). We've seen the importance of choice of words; and now the importance of good syntax. What, then, of punctuation?

Punctuation is, primarily, the tool of good syntax. When you come to consider *style*, you will see how *individual* style, or call it the writer's voice, is bound up with the *individuality* of the matter expressed. Thus this individuality must inevitably be reflected also in use of syntax. It must then also be reflected in the use of punctuation.

When you have learned the rules, and when you have lived with them so long that you no longer notice their presence, then you will be qualified to break them.

Consideration

1. Consider the dictionary meaning of *spell* and *speil* and *gospel*, and relate the meaning to what you understand by 'the writer's responsibility'. Why are the people referred to in the quotation from J.S. Mill (page 58) unlikely to become good writers?
2. What is meant by 'the satirist's twist' in reference to the quotation from Alexander Pope in this chapter?
3. Consider the revised version of the student's poem about the slug (page 59). Is it an improvement? What for instance, do you feel about the line, 'plucked without a thought by my hand'? Do hands have thoughts?

Suggestions for Practice

1. Rewrite the sentences from newspapers which are quoted in this chapter. Altering the syntax to give the meaning the writers intended.
2. Choose from one of your previous compositions a paragraph. See if you can improve it by simply altering the syntax.
3. Make your own collection of examples of fine syntax.

Chapter Eight

SOUND AND COLOUR

So far we have suggested two gifts essential to the fine writer. The command of words, and the command of syntax. But there is a third: The command of music. 'The man,' says Coleridge, 'that hath not music in his soul can indeed never be a genuine poet.' Nor ever, he might have added, a memorable writer.

The truth is, of course, that the gift is single. And cutting it up like this we must be careful — we mustn't become the mad professor who cut up the nightingale to find the song. So let's say that the third *element* of the gift is the gift of music.

Now we can get on with the operation. We'll cut the music in two, into *rhythm* and *sound*. And while we're at it we'll give rhythm a good shake, so that *metre* falls clean away.

Rhythm and Metre

Look at these first lines of four sonnets:

One day I wrote her name upon the strand . . .

Spenser

When in the chronicle of wasted time . . .

Shakespeare

Earth has not anything to show more fair . . .

Wordsworth

one's not half two. It's two are halves of one . . .

e. e. cummings.

By turning a deaf ear to them you can read them all by the clock: te-tum te-tum te-tum te-tum te-tum . . . That way you can tell that no man has cheated. They've been true to the sonnet metre. But now go back and read them alive. Can your ear catch how each has a different tune? A different mood? A different enchantment? Of them all, the nearest to the inane, monotonous insistence of te-tum

64

te-tum . . . is the first. And yet it is neither insistent nor monotonous. Some musical control, the fine edge of a great poet's ear, allows the rhythm to run close to the metre, and so somehow to achieve a tone of heroic solemnity, like a bell tolling somewhere in a fitful wind.

But look at the others. How the *rhythm*, taken from the living voice, runs all awry from the *metre*. In Shakespeare's, with the word 'chronicle' the metre splinters like a pane of glass; and in that shock is the music and the heart-catch of his rhythm.

Look how in the Wordsworth his rhythm holds back from and then runs into the word 'anything', and so achieves the stammer, or almost a sigh, of wonder. And in the cummings look at the truculence of the four equally-stressed syllables of the opening — as if just daring you to think *his* pun the lowest form of wit.

But above all look how in each case the rhythm is the *measure* (and that's one pun to us) of the individual ear.

I do not mean to write blank verse again. Not having the music of rhyme, it requires so close an attention to the pause and the cadence, and such a peculiar mode of expression, as render it, to me at least, the most difficult species of poetry that I have ever meddled with.

William Cowper

Four sonnets — is this rhythm then something confined to verse? Read this:

Have not poetry and music arisen, as it seems, out of the sounds the enchanters made to help their imagination to enchant, to charm, to bind with a spell themselves and the passer-by?

Now go back and read that again. Only this time not for the sense, but for the rhythm. Do you catch it, the dreamy pattern of sound, a wavering pulse that complements so exactly the sense? And perhaps not surprising: it was written by the greatest enchanter of the century, W.B. Yeats. Perhaps then you feel we use too easy an example. All right, then read this:

For, as when the red-cheeked, dancing girls, April and May, trip home to the wintry, misanthropic woods; even the barest, ruggedest, most thunder-cloven old oak will at least send forth some few green sprouts, to welcome such glad-hearted visitants; so Ahab did, in the end, a little respond to the playful allurings of that girlish air.

65

No comment. *You* decide whether the six hundred pages of *Moby Dick* are poetry or prose.

Rhythm is inescapable. Its sense is as much a part of us as our heartbeat. And just as it is virtually impossible to walk without rhythm, so it is impossible to speak without rhythm. In fact the rhythm of speech is part of its expression. In the end the mystery comes back to that *individuality*.

Anyone whose room, say at college, has been one of many in a long corridor will have come by this mystery. Very soon he will have recognized each neighbour just by the sound of his footsteps. Walking is about the commonest achievement; how then does it lend itself to being so endlessly individual? Our use of language runs on the same mystery.

Learning to play the piano, we may school ourselves with a metronome — and in that way, as it were, gain command of the metre. But if we become fine pianists we interpret the composer's *rhythms* in the measure of our own. That is how we bring to the music our own authority. It also explains how no two fine pianists will make the same of a piece of music.

As writers we choose a metre for some particular purpose. Byron for instance chose that of the thunder of horsemen as being appropriate to his poem, 'The Destruction of Sennacherib':

The Assyrian came down like a wolf on the fold,
And his cohorts were gleaming in purple and gold . . .

But if we write by metre alone we are *dictated* to. And that means we have no authority and have surrendered our individuality. In fact what one comes to see is that language does not even lend itself to strict metre. Words are too varied in sound and colour and strength. It may even be that, like all other things, no two words *are* of exactly the same weight (dot and clot — try it on the ear). And even the same word — no two of us will make the same of it; the colour and nuance will depend on our individual accent or dialect — it will even depend on our age, our size and our state of health. No, words lend themselves only to rhythm.

The writer knows that if he wishes to be lively he must express by means of his own authority, his own voice. His problem then is to impose on his chosen metre (whether in prose or in verse) the vibrancy and life of his own rhythms.

And he has another problem. We've all, if alive to rhythm, had the experience of being moved by the sound of a piece of writing, but then of having at the end no idea of what it has been about. So knowing what we do of the writer's responsibility, we can now see that one aspect of his art is to match the expression of his rhythm to the gist of his meaning. No good labouring all night for the sense of your drinking song, to find in the morning your rhythm's that of a dirge.

It's the art of the demagogue to stir the senses with wonderful sound, which merely disguises the bitter meaning in the small print.

Ezra Pound wrote:

> Rhythm — I believe in an 'absolute rhythm', a rhythm, that is, in poetry which corresponds exactly to the emotion or shade of emotion to be expressed. A man's rhythm must be interpretative, it will be, therefore, in the end, his own, uncounterfeiting, uncounterfeitable.

Sound

If you recite aloud the five vowels, A E I O U, you do something in a sense similar to painting on a piece of paper the seven colours of the spectrum. You mark the cardinal points in a circle of possibility.

The comparison of vowel-sounds with colours is a useful one. Vowel-sounds in writing, as colours in painting, whether used singly or in blend with one another, are capable of similar magical evocation of mood.

A piece of writing (poem or memo or letter) that has no variety of sound is colourless and dull. It is like a landscape on a gloomy day, or under the intense unrelieved sunlight of a mid-summer noon. Colourful writing, on the other hand, is like the landscape you find in bright Spring with the cloud well-broken and shifting — in other words, alive with the variety of colour and the interplay of brilliant highlights and shadows. Except that its colours aren't colours, they are sounds.

The master-writer is one who knows instinctively how to match the colour of sound to the mood he would create. Look at these two extracts from Wilfred Owen:

> Move him in the sun —
> Gently its touch awoke him once,
> At home, whispering of fields unsown.
> Always it woke him, even in France,
> Until this morning and this snow.
> If anything might rouse him now
> The kind old sun will know.

and

> What passing-bells for these who die as cattle?
> Only the monstrous anger of the guns.
> Only the stuttering rifle's rapid rattle
> can patter out their hasty orisons.

Someone could write a book about the use of sound in either one of those. But in brief, note in the first the hushed o's and u's and the short i's that give the quiet and tenderness to the first lines; and how in the last couplet the whine of the two lone i's in 'might' and 'kind' introduce a sinister apprehension. In the second, see how a terrible bitter anger and grief is set in the interplay of the rasping short a's and the squealing i's.

> In lyric poetry, language, from being a utensil, or a medium of traffic and barter passes back to its place among natural sounds; its affinity is with the wind among the rocks; it is the cry of the heart, as simple as the breath we draw, and as little ordered with a view to applause. Yet speech grew up in society, and even in the most ecstatic of its uses may flag for lack of understanding and response.
>
> Prof. Walter Raleigh

Of course he doesn't get his effect simply by his use of vowels. There are the consonants too (in the second, most obviously, the r's and the t's); then the rhythm, and the way that matches the mood — and the meaning . . .

Devilish difficult this business of writing! No, not really. Because with much practice all the senses learn to comply. When you start to drive a car you can tie your brain up in a cat's cradle if you try and remember for each foot and hand its special duties. But after a bit — the hell with it! You just get in and drive. All the same, you don't just *get* to be a good driver. Not without practice, and the gift or the knack. It's the same with writing.

Sound Devices

How useful if we could find one quotation that would illustrate all the devices of sound that are worth a mention. Try Shakespeare. Open the book and here are the first lines that present themselves:

> Aye, but to die, and go we know not where,
> To lie in cold obstruction, and to rot;
> This sensible warm motion to become
> A kneaded clod; and the delighted spirit
> To bathe in fiery floods; or to reside
> In thrilling regions of thick-ribbed ice.

1. Rhyme

Some of us are brought up to believe that rhyme *is* poetry. That's nonsense of course. We employ rhyme merely to bring colour and shape to verse. But there's verse, and there's free verse, and neither is *necessarily* poetry.

The rhyme usually falls at the end of the line.

> I'se got a nickel, you's got a dime,
> You buy de coke an' I'll buy de wine.

Is that a rhyme? No, in fact it's what's called a half-rhyme. But nothing wrong with that, if that's what you intend.

There's also internal rhyme. Not so obvious, but it does just the same thing. Listen how subtly Shakespeare enlivens that first couplet above with hidden rhyme: Ay, die, lie; go and know; not and rot.

2. Assonance

This is simply a correspondence of sound between words and syllables. *Correspondence* is good here because of the implication that the words in this way keep in touch. It is thus that the tune is sustained; or even a number of tunes, played in counterpoint.

Look at the Shakespeare again. There are two main themes, the 'i' theme and the 'o' theme. Read it aloud and listen how they play against each other. A thing that is beautiful is the way the 'i' theme is established at the beginning in 'staccato' of pure rhyme; then later it is reintroduced, but now muted in mere assonance (delight, reside, ice) to ring like an echo. Listen also for the minor theme of the e's in lines 1, 4 and 6. But finally what is wonderful is that when one reads great writing each sound is *telling* and seems set absolutely true. True to the mood, the drama, and the tune.

It is as almost impossible to escape from assonance as from rhythm; and assonance is similarly capable of infinite subtlety and effect. Spenser again:

> Your string shall soone to sadder tenor turn
> And tech the woodes and waters to lament.

What magic! The sound seems to evolve to some logic of its own. It's like listening to a stream; you hear the surface babbling — but there's something else you half think you hear, undercurrents of sense and music.

You can, of course, have *dissonance* too: putting sounds side by side that grate together. A student came up proud with this staggering line:

> Stark as stray dog baying in a pitch black cave.

He had agonized for hours. Was baying really more inspired than barking? and what about dark for black? Or bitch for dog? Or whelp yelping?

Decisions, they are maddening.

3. *Alliteration*

All these devices, when pointed out in literature, we tend to look at in some wonder. But in fact we grow up with them, and command them naturally in our daily speech. When you shout, 'Don't you dare do that!' you've used alliteration (those words beginning with 'd'), and quite unconsciously to give explosive emphasis to your command.

'The soft sighing of the sea . . .' Yes, alliteration is probably the easiest employed of all. But what about:

> The sound comes to me
> Of the lapsing, unsoilable,
> Whispering sea.
>
> Oliver St. John Gogarty

Like everything else, alliteration *can* be used with extraordinary subtlety. It may even be that you have to look really closely at that piece of Shakespeare's above before you notice his superb alliteration. Before we point it out, have a try.

In fact it runs right through it. First hinted at by the little word 'to' — to die, to lie, to rot. But then in the last two lines suddenly it extends itself and blossoms, the 't' *and* the 'r':

> . . . *t*o *r*eside
> In *t*hrilling *r*egions of *t*hick-*r*ibbed ice.

4. *Onomatopoeia*

You remember that line of Tennyson's '. . . and murmur of innumerable bees'? That's onomatopoeia. Words whose sounds imitate or echo the sound they describe. THUD, SQUELCH, CLATTER AND WHINE. Obvious enough. But by now we should be looking past the obvious to the subtle and artful. We've talked of the colours of sound, and of how sound is descriptive of mood. So now we can say that in all fine writing the sound itself is expressive; in fact that in all good writing there is an element of onomatopoeia.

Here is a line of prose chosen quite at random from Charles Dickens:

> It was as if the wind and rain had lulled at last after a long and fearful storm.

70

Now try to claim that rhythm, assonance, alliteration and onomatopoeia are properties exclusive to verse.

The Art Concealed

The inexperienced writer, excited by language and its possibilities, tends to keep at his elbow a list of devices and figures of speech. Most often he uses them self-consciously and for their own sake. That means that the reader is aware of him, and his self-consciousness, and his devices — and less aware of what he is trying

---

Bjorn Asbrandsson was a famous warrior, besides being a great poet to boot, like all wanderers from Iceland. Although he was somewhat drunk, he managed to improvise some highly skilful verse in King Harald's honour in a metre known as Toglag. This was the latest and most difficult verse-form that the Icelandic poets had invented, and indeed his poem was so artfully contrived that little could be understood of its contents. Everybody, however, listened with an appearance of understanding, for any man who could not understand poetry would be regarded as a poor specimen of a warrior.

Frans G. Bengtsson

---

to say. The fully accomplished writer on the other hand is so sure of his voice that he can forget himself. And he is so practised in *his* use of the devices that they now just fall into place. The reader is not distracted by them — perhaps not even aware of them — because they are not in any way apart from what is being expressed.

A student had begun his training with a writer. After a few days, confident of his new prowess, he came up with a piece of work. The writer read it. He then took a scrap of paper, wrote on it and handed it to the student.

ARS EST CELARE ARTEM

The student blushed. He had just enough Latin to know that meant: The art is to conceal the art.

Suggestion for Practice

1. Choose a sonnet. Discuss first whether its metre is true. Then discuss how, if at all, the poet's rhythm breaks with the metre. And to what effect?

71

2. Write sentences in which the sound is appropriate to the sense:
   (a) A jet at take-off
   (b) A fire on a still frosty evening
   (c) A stream in a wood — in summer/then in winter
3. Find and/or write your own examples of:
   (a) Half-rhyme
   (b) Alliteration
   (c) Hidden or internal rhyme
   (d) Assonance
   (e) Onomatopoeia

Chapter Nine

DEFINITIONS

So there is writing, but there is also the *craft* of writing: and that is something which we, as writers, must all practise. But for each of us, where the art goes from there, there is no knowing.

The poem, the story (any work of art), it is an adventure — which by origin means 'a coming towards'. If we knew beforehand precisely how it would turn out we would in all likelihood never begin! In a sense the piece would have already been written. In Cervantes' *Don Quixote* there is an encounter with a painter. He is asked what he is

> Mauve takes offence at my having said, 'I am an artist' — which I do not take back, because the word of course included the meaning: always seeking without absolutely finding. It is just the converse of saying, 'I know it, I have found it.'
>
> As far as I know that word means: 'I am seeking, I am striving, I am in it with all my heart.'
>
> Vincent Van Gogh

painting. 'That,' he says, 'is as it may turn out to be.' That says it all: the artist's paradox, his authority *and* his dependence; the need, the exploration, and integral with both, as we saw with Hopkins and his wave, the mystery of self definition.

Much moonshine surrounds the popular idea of the writer and his life. Where this leads to unfounded aspiration, it leads also to disillusionment, dejection and despair. There are definitions, then, which it is important to get straight from the start.

The Artist

Art, says the dictionary, is skill as a result of knowledge and practice.

That all? That's all. Whenever one makes or performs something with skill, and with concern for its excellence, one is an artist. It is quite difficult to think of any activity that is not susceptible to the devotion of skill, and which therefore may not qualify one as an artist. One can be an artist in the conduct of virtually every department of one's life. 'The artist,' Ananda Coomaraswamy wrote in a famous aside, 'is not a special kind of man, but every man is a special kind of artist.'

> All creation or passage of non-being into being is poetry or making, and the processes of all art are creative; and the masters of arts are all poets or makers.
>
> Plato

A person who can write his name has already made significant progress in the art of writing.

Form

Form is the most elementary, simple, crucial, and exacting concern of the creative artist.

A screwdriver is a screwdriver because it is a screwdriver — and if it came in the form of a pipe-cleaner it would be a useless screwdriver. A good screwdriver is a *good* screwdriver. And that's as near as I can get to explaining Gertrude Stein's famous quip, 'a rose is a rose is a rose'. In other words the form of a thing *is* what it is.

A writer learns that the choice of form is his first concern. If he has an idea for a television serial and tries to give it the form of a sonnet something is going to be wrong somewhere. Or rather, everything is going to be wrong everywhere.

Ezra Pound again:

Form. — I think there is a 'fluid' as well as a 'solid' content, that some poems may have form as a tree has form, some as water poured into a vase. That most symmetrical forms have certain uses. That a vast number of subjects cannot be precisely, and therefore not properly rendered in symmetrical form.

In other words the form of what you have to say is what you have to say.

Slant

You have an idea for a story. How will you tell it?

You can make yourself the hero and narrate it in the first person; or you can keep yourself out of it and tell it in the third person: they, he and she.

You can set it in the past, present or future.

You can tell it briefly or at great length.

You can treat the story as a matter of fact, or earnestly, or humorously, or satirically.

You can tell it all in dialogue, or use no dialogue at all.

You can exaggerate, or understate, or write of things exactly as they are.

You can choose to know your characters only by what they do in the story, or you can choose to know everything about their lives, their thoughts and their secrets.

You can tell the story in true sequence, or you can use 'flash-backs' and memories to make a nonsense of time.

And so on.

Each choice involves the artist in a deliberate decision; and together they will constitute the *slant*.

Every piece of writing, poetry or prose, long or short, is subject to slant.

Writing 'At First Hand'

Two accounts of the same incident:

(1) The old man spent some time getting the fire going again. When finally it caught, he muttered something to the youngster.

(2) Old Jack raked the cinders together with a piece of cardboard and spread them judiciously over the whitening dome of coals. When the dome was thinly covered his face lapsed into darkness but, as he set himself to fan the fire again, his crouching shadow ascended the opposite wall and his face slowly re-emerged into light. It was an old man's face, very bony and hairy. The moist blue eyes blinked at the fire and the moist mouth fell open at times, munching once or twice mechanically when it closed. When the cinders had caught he laid the piece of cardboard against the wall, sighed and said; 'That's better now, Mr O'Connor.'

James Joyce

The first account is merely *reportage*; it tells what happened. But the second conjures the action; it has it happen here and now before our eyes. This is writing 'at first hand'. It is a knack. Some are born with it, but most young writers tend to reportage — and there are some, even quite good writers who never acquire the knack. Usually the knack comes as with practice the writer's ear develops. Often it requires guidance.

Only by writing at first hand can one *breathe life* into one's work — and life, as by now you will concede, is particular.

Jargon

One would need to be arrogant or stupid to suppose another will trouble with what one has written if one has not been at pains to express it as well as one is able.

. . . it de-mystifies all competitive, other-directed standards of self-evaluation, until, at last, people grow fiercely restive with the massification on which industrial institutions are based.

Sometimes, especially with the use of jargon, bad writing is a pretension, it is the trumping up of a good resonance of phoney language to give the impression of authority.

> Words are, of course, the most powerful drug used by mankind.
>
> Rudyard Kipling

What is jargon?

. . . the two main vices of jargon? The first is that it uses circumlocution rather than short straight speech. It says, 'In the case of John Jenkins deceased, the coffin' when it means 'John Jenkin's coffin': and its yea is not yea, neither is its nay nay: but its answer is in the affirmative or the negative, as the foolish and superfluous 'case' may be. The second vice is that it habitually chooses vague woolly abstract nouns rather than concrete ones.

That is from one of Sir Arthur Quiller-Couch's Lectures On the Art of Writing. He might have mentioned a third main vice, the facile use of the catch-phrase of the day: 'the on-going situation', 'at this moment in time'. If the pointers are time-honoured, so it would appear are the pitfalls. Unless a person has toiled his thoughts to their clearest, most apparently effortless expression, those thoughts have not been thought through. Thoughts vaguely expressed are vague thoughts.

Quiller-Couch concludes his lecture like this:

If your language be jargon, your intellect, if not your whole character, will almost certainly correspond. Where your mind should go straight, it will dodge: the difficulties it should approach with a fair front and grip with a firm hand it will be seeking to evade or circumvent. For the Style is the Man, and where a man's treasure is there his heart, and his brain, and his writing, will be also.

Archaism

Archaism is a subsection of jargon. The bad or lazy writer often thinks he can fool the reader with his work if he garbs it with the learnedness of antiquity or the piousness of *Hymns Ancient and Modern* or the poeticality of Palgrave. He writes lest for unless, and the sun shone forth for the sun came out, and automobile for car.

The writer, finally, is vital because by using the language of the moment he is witness to the living.

Conviction and Delight

Have you ever had the experience of trying to conceal in a letter to a boy-friend or a girl-friend that your interest in him or her has gone cold? It can't be done. Very mysterious — you can cudgel your heart and quote *The Song of Songs*, but they'll know. Words are very honest — and very treacherous.

So don't be surprised that nobody wants to read your stuff if you yourself didn't very much want to write it. Don't expect to convince anyone if you yourself have no conviction. No matter what your motive for writing, if it does not include delight, then you can be sure your writing is a bore.

The First Draft

So you are ready to make a start. How clean and cold is that white sheet of paper. Yes, we all know the feeling.

Any writer who has not been writing for a while feels 'rusty'. Rusty — and so is his writing, like the water that comes out of a tap that's not been used all winter. So you run the tap, and in a while the water comes clear.

Get writing then, and know that once the words are down you can see them and begin to work and worry them. The first draft is almost always the trail-blazer; permanent track will follow later.

Alan Sillitoe once said:

A writer's first draft is always his safety net; in that he can safely write whatever comes, trusting that it may be of use somehow. But if the first draft is written on talent, the second is a produce of art; it is at this stage that he will need all his wits and independence to remain true to what he has.

Or as the quip has it, 'Get it writ, then get it right.'

The Muse

She exists. We should say no more about her.

Originality and 'The Writer's Voice'

What do you understand by the word 'original'? 'He's an original writer.' It seems to have come to mean something like 'unusual' or 'novel' or just 'different'. And this, since the word is used as a term of praise, is misleading.

In fact the word means something else altogether. An original artist is one who encounters the origin of his work within his *individual* experience of the imagination. It is this authentic experience that affords his work the conviction of absolute authority — or in other words, its originality. What is original must be individual — in that sense it *is* different.

We have talked about a writer finding his voice. Let us be clear exactly what is meant by this. A writer can say with real authority only what he alone has to say; i.e. only when he is being original. But he can only know what *he* has to say when, as a writer, he is self-assured; in other words he finds his real voice when he finds himself. What this implies is unnerving? It implies that the quality of the work cannot be divorced from the quality of the life.

Scholarship and Criticism

Scholars must go their own way; and the critics will certainly go theirs. That's fine. The writer knows by his scars all too well that there is such a thing as criticism. But he also knows that in the world he serves, the world whose greatest mystery is its variety, there is no 'absolute' criticism. What gives criticism authority is the same as that which gives writing authority — exact individual response.

All criticism is a matter of taste. We listen to it, good or bad; but finally we must believe in ourselves.

Is it Important to be Published?

If you're a fine cobbler it's your concern to make good shoes. You make them well, and that is your satisfaction. They wear well and are comfortable and that is a satisfaction to others; and their satisfaction gives you an added satisfaction. If you made the most beautiful pair of shoes in the world, would you want them to be worn, or to be put in a museum?

If you're an explorer, and finally, having risked your life many times, you find the source of the longest river, which, for you, is the moment of satisfaction? The moment of discovery, or the moment of your return when you tell the world of your achievement? Did you make the discovery for yourself or for the world?

If you discover a cure for cancer, what is your satisfaction: the discovery, or the publication of the discovery, or the fact of seeing people cured? Or all three?

If you were a visionary, and had a family to support, would you market your visions, or would you say, 'No, these are too holy, I will not demean them by bringing them into the market-place.' And go out and get a job.

Can you imagine being a writer and saying: 'These things of mine, they seem quite mysterious, almost to have been *given* to me. Perhaps then I owe it to them and to other people to do what I can to get them published.'?

Or else of saying this: 'I am a professional writer, I live by my work and that is my dignity. The proof of my work's value is that it makes me a living and so enables me to work some more. If my work isn't published it has failed.'?

Or else this: 'A human-being is a social animal. For him the act of making something is unfinished until the fact and the need of its existence have been confirmed by another human's response. Until my work is published as far as I am concerned it does not exist.'?

Or this: 'If I don't get my stuff published then neighbours think I'm just a layabout. But if I do get it published then they sort of respect me — and they're keen to have me at their parties. Not that they read my books.'

Or even this: 'My writing is a private celebration of my being alive. I write, and as well as I can, because that's what being alive means to me. Publication? It's neither here nor there.'?

> So far as I am individually concerned, and independent of my pocket, it is my earnest desire to write those sort of books which are said to 'fail'.
>
> Herman Melville

So it is important to be published? You answer. After all, you are the only one who *can* tell you.

But, if it's any help, here are two things that publication will never do. First, it will never prove that you are any good as a writer. Second, it will not even prove that you are a writer.

If you look to publication for such proof, then watch out: you're a very inflammable moth, the one in the legend who is consumed by the flame of his own illusion.

In the first place, no writer ever knows whether he is any damn good. In the second place, there is for the writer only one proof of identity that is meaningful and incontrovertible: the strange evidence that he continues to write.

Suggestions for Practice

Practise . . . . . .